THE

Journey

BACK TO

Balance

An Intentional Path

LISA SOLTERBECK, LCSW, CHT, INTUITIVE EMPATH

BALBOA.
PRESS

A DIVISION OF HAY HOUSE

Balboa Press books may be ordered through booksellers or by contacting:

Balboa Press
A Division of Hay House
1663 Liberty Drive
Bloomington, IN 47403
www.balboapress.com
1 (877) 407-4847

Because of the dynamic nature of the Internet, any web addresses or links contained in this book may have changed since publication and may no longer be valid. The views expressed in this work are solely those of the author and do not necessarily reflect the views of the publisher, and the publisher hereby disclaims any responsibility for them.

The author of this book does not dispense medical advice or prescribe the use of any technique as a form of treatment for physical, emotional, or medical problems without the advice of a physician, either directly or indirectly. The intent of the author is only to offer information of a general nature to help you in your quest for emotional and spiritual well-being. In the event you use any of the information in this book for yourself, which is your constitutional right, the author and the publisher assume no responsibility for your actions.

Any people depicted in stock imagery provided by Thinkstock are models, and such images are being used for illustrative purposes only.
Certain stock imagery © Thinkstock.

Print information available on the last page.

ISBN: 978-1-5043-7952-6 (sc)
ISBN: 978-1-5043-7954-0 (hc)
ISBN: 978-1-5043-7953-3 (e)

Library of Congress Control Number: 2017906895

Balboa Press rev. date: 01/25/2018

ABOUT

This book is my unique story of how I worked from my wounded self to my balanced state of being. I was determined to heal from the inside out. I documented each step of the way so I could help others find their way back home to a balanced self. I didn't do what was traditional to healing; I did what worked. May this book find those who need a new way and share the wisdom I learned from my journey. I want to help you find your balance, your place of peace. Your disturbed state is a reminder that you need to heal from inside out. Get ready to let go and come home.

DEDICATION

I dedicate this book to all those who have been wounded by trauma and thrown off course from their true destiny.

ACKNOWLEDGEMENTS

I am grateful for the many wonderful people in my life who have offered me their support and inspiration. Without them, this book would not have been possible.

First and foremost, I want to thank my partner Torrii for encouraging me along every step of my path and helping me cultivate a life that brings love to the world. I also want to thank my two sons Austin and Taylor, and all of my family and friends that believed in my ability to be more. Each one of them saw me struggle and suffer by living an unbalanced life. Through their love and desire for me to be true to myself, I was able to find the strength to transform my chaos into a much more streamlined life that creates health, wellness and authentic fulfillment. Thank you for believing in me even when I couldn't see it. I love you all!!

Next, to my wise teachers and mentors, for all the gifts that they have shared with me: Larry Dillenbeck – Lighthouse Center for Consciousness Studies HypnoTherapy & NLP Certifications; Gary and Sharon Morris – I Am Awake, Accelerated Awakenings & Parts Work Training; Kathleen Braza – Death and Dying; Dr. Jerry Braza – Mindfulness Training, Relationships and Love; and to all of my college and university professors.

Finally, I would like to give a special thank you to Brian Schmidt, Lori Welborn, Alex Douglas and the entire team at Journeys... A Center for Your Soul, for their contributions to and support for this book.

CONTENTS

FOREWORD

Life is a question of balance. Moment by moment we are dancing with ourselves trying to stay grounded or afloat, despite our busyness and the challenges we face. One's health, life, and happiness always come back to how we maintain our personal and collective balance. It is determined by how we navigate the waves of life.

A favorite story of mine is called "duck meditation," popularized by meditation teacher Tara Brach. Imagine a duck rolling back and forth on the waves of the ocean. The duck survives because it doesn't resist the waves; instead it rests atop each ebb and flow. Since she is not worried about the immensity of the ocean she finds peace. Meanwhile, at a deeper level the duck recognizes that she is more than a duck on a wave—she is one with the water and ocean. You might say that we are all like that duck. As we attempt to keep above water, we also realize that there is something greater; the ocean, the sun, the moon, the stars, the entire universe—spirit!

Through years as a psychotherapist and workshop presenter, Lisa Solterbeck has learned how to be a true compass for those who are challenged by the waves of life. As a result of her direct experience, she has created a holistic model that offers a reminder of how to return to your own resources to heal and grow as you navigate your relationship with self and others.

Her process is called "Essence Illumination" — a soul journey that moves a person beyond ego into a sense of their true self. This book offers you, the reader, an opportunity to go deeper into your interior by offering multiple ways to help you return to your true essence, which is love. As you slowly take in this message, you will realize that you are never alone and that you are always connected to the entire Universe, God or Spirit or whatever word helps you to understand the ultimate dimension. This book will guide you in discovering a workable template to help you to look deeply and — "find your way back to a true state of balance, one that allows you to be free to follow your instincts and your desires."

As the author of *Moment by Moment: The Art and Practice of Mindfulness* and *The Seeds of Love: Growing Mindful Relationships* and as a spiritual guide, I resonate with these wonderful teachings. Like "dharma rain" they will slowly enter your consciousness and become a guide for you to live your life more fully and awake. It will become a resource that you will be able to return to on a daily basis for reminders that will illuminate your journey and help you to flow with the waves and become one with the ocean.

Jerry Braza, Ph.D.
Author, Dharma Teacher and Spiritual Guide
Contact Information: www.theseedsoflove.net

INTRODUCTION

Do you ever feel lost trying to find the purpose and meaning of random events in your life? Do you live in fear, eager to do whatever you can to find peace? Are you packing your life with artificial fillers like unhealthy relationships and pointless distractions? It's time to unravel the drama in your life and return to who you are.

As you find yourself moving deeper and deeper into self-destruction and self-sabotage, the great urgency of this task of discovery seems obvious. But many people don't know where to start, much less what set of actions will move them back to a healthy, fulfilled life.

Through my professional practice, I've been privileged and honored to work with some amazing people, helping them to unravel their tangled lives and heal their wounded and trapped souls. Most of their problems stem from accepting society's conditioning. I have found some simple strategies that can awaken the spirit and bring peace to those caught in the rough seas of life.

Don't misunderstand: the purpose of this book is not to remove the rough seas or erase the difficult journey you may be on. That's not what I do. I want to help you see how the missteps of your journey can lead you to become the great captain of your own ship.

I'm reminded of the African proverb, "Smooth seas never made a skillful sailor." That simple saying holds a hidden gift of truth that helps us see our actual goal. We're not here to fix the sea, though we may affect it; we're here to improve our skills as a sailor. That certainly reframes the questions!

Can you imagine? Everything that has happened in your journey is just exactly what you need to turn your wounded self into a flourishing successful self! Who knew?

If you're ready to turn rough seas into the adventure of a lifetime, then pull up a chair, grab a warm cup of tea and let's get to it. Together, we'll start planning for the unpredictable undertaking ahead. The adventure will lead to new territory, so being prepared is crucial to the success of the journey.

Of course, we'll need to talk about a few concepts, starting with **balance**, which I define as:

> The distribution of one's life in such a way that it enables you to remain upright and steady, no matter the external condition. To put life in an order or priority that will allow for optimal buoyancy and maximum potential for growth.

So when I speak of balance, I'm referring to a way of life where your sense of peace isn't ripped away from you when challenges and strife come into your world. Life is, after all, a continuous series of ups and downs, and it is important to know how to use our great gifts to transform this motion into positive growth.

The concept of **growth** is a good framework for us to use to begin this journey. Growth indicates life and health. So, we'll spend some time focusing on how to grow regardless of adversity.

And of course we need to understand **adversity**. I think we all understand the struggle to find moments of peace in the midst of chaos. I like to use the metaphor of a ship going through stormy seas to help illustrate the situation and the actions we'll need to take.

Throughout this process I will teach you three important skills:

1) How to determine when you are out of balance, or (continuing the ship metaphor) how to know your ship is sinking.
2) How to return to your core, or how to come back to the dock to get proper fuel, repairs, and resources to continue.
3) How to move toward your heart's desires through conscious action, or how to plot and stay on course for your created purpose.

Ultimately, you will learn how to manage and maintain a state of conscious balance throughout your life experiences. That's not to say you won't be tested from time to time. You'll need to do some readjusting now and then. I want to teach you how to ride out these challenges and regain your desired state by just being aware of when and how you are out of balance.

When we finish this exploration, you will *know* who you are, *trust* who you are, and—without equivocation—stay *true* to your authentic self. This is true homeostasis! If you understand that the goal of balance is being in complete alignment with your higher self, then you'll do what you were created to do: be true to your authentic self. No person or event can ever knock you off your mark.

If you're excited to get started, this might be a good point to skip ahead to Chapter 1. But if you're still not sure about this book or me or what this might mean for you, let me explain further and give you some personal insights I've learned along the way.

One thing I know from my years as a therapist is that individuals who believe they have no choice end up living like they have no choice. If an individual is wounded and hurting, they tend to act out that hurt. It never ends.

Maybe this will sound familiar. It begins with a traumatic event in which your ability to take action is missing, not because you were wounded in the past, but because you are in "fight, flight or freeze" mode and your brain chose "freeze" because it was just trying to survive the moment. But later in life, when your brain is re-stimulated by a similar event, you have the same non-response. And you're stuck! That's how easy it happens.

And how do I know this? Well, when I was a little girl and faced with abuse, I felt wounded and helpless to create the life I wanted. For much of my early years, I truly believed, at my core, that I was not *able* to make choices that would lead to love. I kept finding myself in the same situation, where the thing that wounded me kept coming back to haunt me. Finally, I realized that the way of healing was a series of my choices. And so I made a choice of love, a choice to do no harm, a choice to choose me, and a choice to move on.

My personal experience convinced me that I would continue to feel lost and trapped until I was able to choose differently. I had to decide to pull the "charge" of trauma out of my body by emoting. I had to choose to shift my beliefs back to truth. I had to choose to move forward from the helpless state of the past and into a more resourceful state that's in the present. This is why there is so much research and teachings on being "in the moment." The present moment is the place where we can make choices and create a new reality, not just one the one that is familiar to you.

I want to give you back the choice to live a great life and to leave "the survivor" in the past—grateful for its gifts, but ready to regain the life you have always deserved.

I've learned that the survivor mentality can easily overshadow your true identity, especially if it becomes your norm. Any state that is repeated regularly becomes a habit that's not easily broken. So just surviving can keep you in survival mode but that's as far as you get – alive but not living to your fullest potential.

Finding out who you are must be of the utmost priority. To waste time is stealing from your spirit's joy and your precious moments.

This just may be the reason you picked this book up! You're thinking to yourself, "I'm not completing my voyage successfully. How can I get my life back on course?" Great question! I'm going to show you the key components of learning how to sail your ship correctly and then you'll be off! I'll map it out, play-by-play, and then you can get back into the ocean. Change is in the air and I can feel success just around the corner!

It might help too if I explain something here about an unseen force I will call "The Universe." This is my attempt to define something BIG and beyond us, that which we can't completely understand or control, the creator of fate and the ultimate game changer. We try to get close to or tap into this Universe "thing" by looking through the lenses of science, religion, spirituality or philosophy. Whatever your definition of this energy, you can apply these principles through that lens.

I believe the Universe is an energy force that we can access and collaborate with, or we can choose to act as if it's not there. But think of the Serenity Prayer:

"God, grant me the serenity to accept the things I cannot change,
Courage to change the things I can,
And wisdom to know the difference."
- *Reinhold Niebuhr (1892–1971)*

It's showing us that a higher power <u>is</u> interrelated to our growth. I want to teach you how to build a relationship with the Universe that is interconnected, like a fine-tuned machine. Great things can be made from that state! When you are disconnected from it, you will feel like a boat without a paddle, looking for purpose and connection.

This unseen force wants to support us in becoming part of our authentic self. It doesn't want to hurt us; it wants to help us. We were created to grow and to become what we were formed to be, so when we don't grow or aren't true to ourselves, the unseen force is affected in a negative way. Every action causes a reaction.

For example, I was created to touch the world with love. If I am destructive to the world in some way, I send a message to the Universe that I am not Lisa Solterbeck. I am an imposter! It will want to shake me off my course just like a dog wants to shake off a flea.

When we aren't in balance, the Universe supports us in a way that is similar to a healthy parent. It sees our behaviors as hurting ourselves. It loves us, but cannot support behaviors that will hurt us or others. It feels pain because we are a part of it and if we are not valuing it, a negative reaction will occur.

It's clear that our outside world reflects our inside world. When we are off center, the Universe waits for us, loves us, supports us, and offers messages and omens to us. If we are willing to pay attention and listen, we can re-adjust and get back on track.

I remember sitting in the dentist office one day, and for the first time in my life, understanding the concept that my outer world was a reflection of my inner world. I was exhausted, broke, and had arrived late for my appointment. I scanned the room and in the right corner was a slightly disheveled young man and next to him was a large, 32-ounce soda sitting on the windowsill, apparently left there by someone else. He picked it up and started to drink it. His mother admonished him and asked what he was doing. He replied "What? It's here."

Then I turned to the doorway and a woman and her husband came running in. She looked worried to death. Her partner supported her as she paced the waiting room floor. Eventually the doctor called her name but informed her that her husband could not join the consultation. She went into a bit of hysterics but agreed and he returned to their car to wait.

Another person was sitting in front of me, tapping their foot in annoyance that they were running behind while yet another patient came in looking for an emergency appointment. After being told that there was no room, they left enraged that they couldn't get in that day, slamming the door behind them.

About five minutes passed and the distressed woman came running back out to the waiting room, demanding to find her husband. As she ran out the door, she tripped and fell, breaking her front tooth! She exclaimed, "THIS IS WHAT HAPPENS WHEN I DON'T HAVE MY HUSBAND!"

In this very moment, I saw "me" as never before: co-dependent with her partner, who really had nothing left except for a someone else's cup of soda to drink, impatient and out of time, and frustrated that the world didn't give her what she wanted. That's when I realized I needed help.

This "holding my whole life together" thing just wasn't working anymore. I realized that I thought only in the past. I thought that was my little secret, but really it was all quite public, playing out like a movie for the whole world to see. I just hadn't seen it for myself. But like recognizes like and the Universe was trying to hold a mirror. I didn't like what I saw. **Lesson learned.**

You may struggle with the feeling that the Universe is withholding good things from you. It's a common mistake. In reality, the Universe is just reminding us to look inward and resolve the errors or mistakes we're making. Until we do, we struggle, until one day we are so out of balance that we feel like we are going to collapse. It's at this point that we are forced to face our deepest fears and explore the parts of our selves that we have been neglecting.

It still amazes me that through the gift of free will we always find the need to come back to truth. I love how we were created to be in balance; we have just been ignoring the messages. Suffering is a direct symptom of being something other than what we were created to be. Each ache in life is a reminder to get back to business!

In the process of adjusting aspects of ourselves that are out of balance, we are given an opportunity to heal, grieve, and let go. This is awakening to the true self. We need to fall in love with those parts of ourselves that have been so greatly neglected and separated from the greater whole of our being.

It's easy to choose to live in a world of denial, anger, blame, and judgment—toward ourselves and others—and never leave our patterns of suffering. That's our comfort zone. It's hard to come back to our center, our set point, where the Universe can meet us and help us find our way to an amazing and fulfilling life. But this is another one of those times where the work is worth doing. This is a degree that can't be earned without completing the course.

As you move through this book, feel free to pause, reflect, and adjust. It's very important that you take the time to fully integrate each concept, and apply and practice them in your daily life. I'm asking you to know this information inside and out, to truly live it, and be able to speak of the lessons you learned after you have completed these steps. You need to be able to "walk your talk" for this work to truly impact your life.

As you choose to work on these areas of your life, you can't help but fall in love with all the unique aspects of yourself and the world around you. When we finally realize that we want more love in our life, we learn to share more love, and it's like a floodgate has opened. The love starts moving you back to your core essence. To be full of love means you can do nothing less than create a beautiful miracle, just as you are a miracle to the Universe.

The goal is to leave no room for anything other than fulfillment. In other words, your goal is to be so full of love that there is no room for fear. This can be defined by the term **effulgence**: to shine forth brilliantly;

to be a radiant light. That can be <u>you</u> in a state of optimal physical, emotional, and mental health.

The first stage of change is understanding the steps that you need to take. The second stage is digesting each concept and mastering it. It will take time. Be willing to put in the effort and take 100% responsibility for your successes and failures. Know that failure is feedback and whatever you invest is what will return to you as an outcome; the results will reflect your effort.

Also keep in mind that if you have been focusing on getting your own way a little too much or you have been too focused on just one area of your life, you are neglecting other essential areas that will need to be explored. I want to help you create a plan for success in <u>all</u> of the areas of your life. Taking your own inventory of these key concepts and then working on each of these areas regularly will allow you to move towards your full capacity as a shining, radiant light.

I have personally made a choice to move toward more love and to progress toward my wholeness for the rest of my life. Love is the state of buoyancy, a necessary aspect to being in balance. You ever notice that feeling of lightness in your heart where everything is good in the world? You have to be connected to love to get that.

Just by picking up this book it's clear that you are ready to make a change in your life. Work hard and don't let anything get in your way. Make it your priority. You can attain a balanced life, one where you are true to your heart's desires. Follow the basic principles in this book and work with the unseen force of the Universe and you too can create the outcome that you desire. Once you have mastered this state I feel confident you won't ever want to let it go.

When you walk your talk, the feeling of being in total alignment will fill you with true unconditional love – a love that can't be contained and must be shared!

So let's begin…

PART ONE

Sonar is a system of sending out sound waves and then listening for the echoed response. It's a concept borrowed from nature, where dolphins and whales use sound and its reflection from distant objects to "see" underwater. Studies have shown these amazing creatures can locate objects as small as a BB pellet up to 50 feet away!

Like dolphins, we use feelings, more than sight, to connect to the world around us. When our "life" ship sends out emotional energy that is confusing, what returns to you in the echo is just as confusing and, worst of all, not an accurate picture of our surroundings.

We want to work with the world around us in a harmonious way. We need to express ourselves clearly and in such a way that our thoughts, feelings, words and actions are all communicating the same message. This is true integrity. If they aren't, the world will misread you and you will see a reflection of a life that is out of harmony with your internal wishes.

Once we understand this goal of integrity, we discover the value of our most precious gift: our inner compass. The inner compass allows us to work with the unconscious and subconscious mind in a way that allows our energetic fields to keep us on course, even when our logical mind would take us off course. Given its importance, we should start any voyage of discovery by understanding our inner compass.

When you feel out of balance, you have (in all probability) turned off the basic human gift of your inner compass. You need to know how to turn it back on. This is one of the most important concepts in this book. Your ability to read and navigate with your compass will be of great benefit to you on your journey back to balance.

The higher self is important here as well. This part of the unconscious sees the higher path and what is in our best interest. We commonly ignore this gift of spiritual knowing and it takes conscious practice to reactive it.

To reconnect the higher self, you will need to sit quietly and ask yourself some basic questions without letting your analytical mind answer. For example: Is there something missing in my life? Do I have needs that I have been ignoring? When the answers come, listen to the quiet, loving voice, not the loud, judgmental one. Use your senses to give you the answers. That may come by sight, sound, or by feeling, but probably not from logical thought.

This takes some practice, but it is a powerful tool to understand the subconscious and its gifts of clarity. The logical mind is limited to what it knows. The higher self holds your map to greatness.

Let's rediscover our inner compass!

CHAPTER ONE

Your Inner Compass

What is an Inner Compass?

We are undergoing a beautiful transformation in human consciousness. Did you know that? We are designed to grow continuously from the inside out, rather than the outside in. But we can become confused and begin to rely entirely on external sources for our sense of ourselves. This creates an imbalance that's hard to overcome. But you can regain your ability to create an inner and outer life that is in perfect alignment. We do this by using our inner compass.

So what do I mean by an inner compass? Well, inside each of us exists a sense that is designed to point to our core truth. In many ways we have been taught to turn off our internal compass or to not trust it at all. We have been trained to listen to the outside world rather than our inside needs and the desires of our core self. In fact, we've been made to feel silly for saying that we "sense" something is off, or suggesting that something doesn't "feel" right. Keep up that kind of talk and you'll eventually be labeled as someone who makes waves or called a troublemaker.

But if you stop listening to this urging from within—if you stop listening to your gut—you will end up in places you never would have chosen. The most likely destination is your past wounds, you know, that sad, familiar territory that you want to avoid more than anything. Your inner compass can direct you toward healthy places.

It's rare that any good comes from misreading a compass. Misreading your inner compass is no exception. So, it takes practice and determination to not compromise or fall back on external feedback. It's not easy to stick to what your compass is telling you and what you've learned along the way. But your compass will become your trusted guide to help you know when you are running your life in or out of balance. To move forward, you need to have a close personal relationship with your inner compass and, even then, it must be continuously fine-tuned.

Learning to Listen to Your Body as a Guide

The body houses your inner compass. The way I know that I am out of balance almost always starts with messages from my body. These messages may arrive as sickness, emotional strain, the inability to focus, a lack of drive, a feeling of disconnect from others, lack of creativity, pain or exhaustion, just to name to few. Once I understood that my body, mind and spirit are all trying to help me, I learned to interpret these messages as opportunities for change. You can do the same!

So many of us forget to check in with our body for data and information. Something feels too constrictive and you know you need to change, but you can't see what that looks like. That's terrifying! And most of us get stuck here. We want to see where we are going before we proceed forward. This can be a major roadblock, because if we are on a spiritual quest or we are growing beyond what we have been taught or have seen in our lifetime, we are going to be sailing blind.

> *To listen to your own internal guide is the only solution to the destiny of your desire. Listening to others sets you on a path of disappointment.*

The only way to navigate this situation is to listen to your body. This process is much like the method of a caterpillar becoming a butterfly. Sometimes you can't see out of the cocoon and you have to tune into the sensations of your body to find your way out. Your body's sensations are the feelings of being out of balance. The feelings are telling you that a change is necessary. This is your inner compass.

When monarch butterflies are migrating, they use the magnetic pull of the earth's poles as a secondary navigation system. They sense the magnetic fields of the earth to make sure they arrive home safe and sound. When butterflies are off course, they are able to sense that they are out of alignment with where they are meant to go and adjust their route accordingly; they "feel" their destiny and let nothing stop them from finding it.

We are similar in many ways. Just like the butterfly, we need and want to fulfill our destiny. And we have numerous messages that are directing us back to our place of balance. What a gift! If we would just start listening more clearly to our pain and discomfort—our feelings of being out of alignment—the world *within* would become illuminated and a state of peace and balance would re-emerge. That sounds yummy to the soul, doesn't it?

The funny thing is that most of us don't even ask what's wrong. Why do I feel this way? Is there something I am not giving myself? How do I get it? Learning to accurately read these messages quickly and effectively can literally be a lifesaver.

We know "dis-ease" in the body can manifest itself into real disease in your body, mind, and/or spirit. So knowing you're in trouble or out of balance is important and the sooner the better. Delaying access to that information would be like not having access to a life preserver until you've hit the bottom of the lake. That's RISKY!

I once had a client who had a serious heart condition, one that was not pre-existing, but manifested suddenly and changed her life drastically. Working with this client for a period of time prior, I knew that she had some unresolved emotional conditions centered on her inability to stand in her self-worth and own her spiritual gifts. Intuitively, I knew this client was a medium, but she was terrified to expose her gifts due to family of origin trauma.

As the health condition worsened, her despair deepened. Then she allowed me to dive deep into her heart and show her how to release the infection. The doorways of her heart opened in front of me. Just like boiling water, the hurts began to evaporate.

Layer by layer, we worked through the chapters of her life that she had sealed up, releasing the pain and freeing her spirit. Like clockwork, as the pain was released, so too were the physical symptoms of her heart condition. We found that when she ignored the hurt, the symptoms would increase and she would be in a medical crisis again.

I'm happy to say that this client is nearing full recovery. By listening to her body and its reminders to stay on course, she has healed both her spiritual and physical heart. This is just one of many cases that I've seen where releasing toxic pain in the emotional body produces a directly correlated result in the physical body.

Tuning Out Negative Self-Talk

So we start by turning on our inner compass. That makes sense. But to be effective we also must turn off the negative self-talk that sabotages our growth. We must stop telling ourselves we really aren't good enough to get our needs and wants met. We need to stop getting angry and believing the world won't meet our needs and wants. We have to stop getting stuck in a victim mentality. If we can't or won't turn off these messages, we can't hear the instructions for healing.

I've come to realize that we can spend our lives waiting, hoping, and praying that someone will tell us that we can move forward by affirming us and reminding us we are good enough. But then, when they pull their approval away for any reason at all, what then? We lash out, judge them, and return to our old wounded self. We just dig a deeper hole. It still amazes me that we think this is the best solution. What trained us to disregard our basic needs and wants and think that emptiness is a normal way of life? My best guess is that **trauma**, the ultimate trickster, taught us this.

If we stick to this pattern, we eventually find ourselves living in a hazy-gray world where we move in and out of a state of trance (a half-conscious state, between awake and asleep). Researchers at Harvard Business School believe that we are only consciously using our brain about 5% of the time, and that 95% of decisions are made from the subconscious and unconscious (Alban, n.d.). Can you imagine how many moments in the **now** we must be missing? Our power to make change is only in the now. If we are in a trance state, living in the future or the past, life is just slipping by. But being in balance allows us to be present, conscious, awake, and alive. In balance, we're able to receive our blessings and to value our birthrights.

One day, my sweet son and his partner said that they wanted to take me to dinner. He was driving and I had the pleasure of being in the passenger seat for once. In this position, as an observer, I noticed my son repeat a pattern I practiced for many years. He happily enjoyed the company but was not paying attention to the necessary route to our destination. Repeatedly he turned in the wrong place, questioning where he should be, and wandering the town as the night passed before us.

It was then I realized that I needed to pick up my car on our way to dinner or I would be stranded on the wrong side of town. He dropped me off, and I got in my car. I was going to follow him to the restaurant across town, when it dawned on me that I was going to be just as misguided as my leader if I didn't wake up. I realized that I must become conscious and find the way on my own. Once I arrived at the restaurant I found that my son took about 10 minutes longer than me to arrive.

I smile when I think back on this. My son was a model of the unconscious driver, focused on other things and shiny objects on the path. It's fine to follow an experienced leader, but if I truly want to be efficient and safe, I need to be conscious and alert. I have to choose the messages I accept about myself and not just cruise along, gulping down negative self-talk. My destiny is my choice.

Breaking Old Habits

I remember the old way. I would suffer and re-live the same unhealthy patterns day after day. If something in my environment scared me, or I believed that a part of me wouldn't be accepted because of shame, fear or something else, I would suppress the impulse to grow. Instead of moving forward, I would hold back the urge to release the energy that had been sparked in me by another. Sadly, I became the prison guard of my own pain.

Now I know that I am the only one who holds the key to break free from this prison. I've learned that letting go is where our true strength lies.

At times it feels like there is no way out, but there is! If you are in the belly of the ship and the waters of suffering start to flood in, get to the ladders and move to the higher levels. To get out you will have to create the rungs of the ladder by living an authentic life. If your thoughts don't match your actions, the rungs won't be strong enough to support you and you will fall into the old wounds of your past. On the other hand, if each aspect of your life leads to the others and your steps make sense with your inner compass, then the Universe will support you. Your thoughts will be in alignment with your feelings and your feelings will be expressed with appropriate words and appropriate actions. Success is guaranteed!

I know this is easier said than done, but it can be done! You have to be brutally honest with yourself and willing to make the change required when you find incongruences between your compass and your life. But isn't this science at its most basic level? Take one step at a time, accepting the truth as you discover it. And our "experiments" must produce consistent results to be accepted. We do that in the laboratory. We should be willing to do it in our lives.

Opening the Heart

Here's something to keep in mind: if we stay in a place of refuge (where we hide to protect ourselves) for too long, it becomes a habit or a norm. If self-protection is not addressed, it becomes a fixed state. The walls you built with your own mind will construct a prison. It will feel like a permanent structure in which you can hide but not escape. To remove yourself from this prison, you must open the doorway of vulnerability and face your fears with courage and an open heart. If the heart is closed with fear, you'll confirm that the prison is the only safe place and you'll feel trapped once again.

As we grow, we must free this energy by releasing the child within, allowing ourselves to fully embrace our true selves, both adult and inner child, becoming one whole being. That is strength, and a balanced self.

This reminds me of a client who consistently overworked herself and never could seem to find time to play. I always tell my clients in this kind of situation that too much duty makes you feel like a "dookie." (Don't ask me where I came up with that term, but everyone seems to innately understand what it means.) This seemed to be just the medicine she needed, but she repeatedly gave me excuses as to why she had to work, to the point of serious over-work and exhaustion, before she played.

I kept reminding her that the Universe doesn't create unhealthy rules like that and explained that overworking is a human condition of programming from childhood. We worked on building play into her life and, instantly, her life began to fall back into balance. From then

Cool note: Carl Jung, the pioneering psychologist, theorized that drive could come from a spiritual instinct and not just from sexual drives, as Sigmund Freud had suggested. Can you see the budding wisdom that was emerging in the early days of psychology? We are more than just human; we are spiritual beings. It's this spiritual drive that can take you to your destiny!

on, any time she noticed the symptom of feeling like a "dookie," she gave herself the medicine of play, and life regained its balance.

If one aspect of our "being" is trapped within the walls of a self-built prison, then all of our actions tend to reflect a victim mentality. We operate from a place of protection, trying not to let anyone see that our behavior is motivated by feelings of inadequacy. Hello, Ms. EGO!

It's true that the ego has a very important job. Its purpose is to keep you safe until you see evidence that it is time to grow again. And it's there to help you identify when the external environment has shifted from danger to safety. The ego is what seeks good for us and tells us when the conditions to thrive have returned. But the ego can also be misled by an inappropriate refusal to be vulnerable and accept the change required for growth. If we let ego run things, it's all about us, but in a way that never actual yields positive results for us.

The Power of Motion

So, making good use of your inner compass is simple. If you find yourself out of balance, slow down and tune in. Remember, as you take each step it's very easy to let your mind play tricks on you and create excuses to sabotage your success. We must all take full responsibility for our thoughts and make the necessary changes to move into full alignment with our greatest state of being. Take one step at a time and you will find that one day you <u>will</u> arrive at your destination – balance and wholeness.

Notice the action words? You must **MOVE** continuously, rhythmically and with love in your heart to heal. Your compass works best when you are in motion. Pausing for self-reflection is necessary, but if the world is to see what a beautiful creature you are, you must get back in motion and bring with you the new aspects of the self you found in your down time. If you need to explore why you have told yourself you cannot go on, you may want to look at where you forgot to let love in. Love is your fuel.

> *For the universe to guide your life, you must remember to keep the mind-body-spirit in motion.*

If fear is in your heart, you will run out of fuel to move forward. True love and beauty must be in motion to be seen by others.

Just as movement is important, so is connectedness. Your compass is valuable for every part of your life, not just one part of your life. Don't be surprised if when you change one aspect of your life, the next aspect is influenced and stimulated. This is the gift: one concept feeds the next and fuels the law of inertia in our lives. Let these seeds of knowledge be planted in your subconscious and allow you to take the action steps required. You will be glad you did when you see the harvest manifested in your life. If the change feels too quick or too scary, slow down and work on what feels manageable. In the end, movement is the key, not how fast it is done.

I was caught by surprise one day when a Catholic nun came to my office for a reading. In the course of our exchange she stated that one thing she had learned from living in the convent was that "love and beauty is always in motion." She continued by saying the love or beauty without motion is just an illusion.

This stirred something inside me and, while I knew it to be true intuitively, I couldn't quite wrap my mind around how to put that into practice. I put a call out to the Universe and said, "Show this to me in a way that I can apply it to my own life." Slowly but surely life started to unravel and I noticed that all the areas of my life that were in a fixed state (trying to be a perfectionist, proving I was right, always needing to make a point, etc.) were all behavior patterns that I had created to say that I had it all figured out. All were ego illusions.

The fact of the matter was that when I used this spiritual test to determine the genuine nature of my actions, I once again came back to the flow of life and was one with all that is. Being humble is a gift; being a know-it-all is exhausting. So being in motion with the flow of life is easier than being in resistance. I know that sounds like a "duh" kind of statement but, wow, that was a hard one for me to learn!

Turning Inward

The inner compass can also tell you things by being silent. Don't be fooled that emptiness always means "something is missing." That void can represent infinite possibilities and a place from which to grow. This is exciting! Don't exchange this excitement for fear. That will kill the potential we find in the inner silence.

If we start anything from fear, we knock over a long chain of dominoes. It's fear that demands that we quickly adopt a persona or a mask so people don't see the vulnerable self. We are afraid something is wrong with us, so we create these identities so the world can be distracted from our inner truth. We are afraid that what is inside us is not good enough and won't be accepted by others. To manage all of that wasted time and energy of self-avoidance, we go into a zone (trance/dissociation) to let time pass without noticing. In doing so, we create a hole inside ourselves, a neglected void in the hull of our ship that allows parasites and barnacles to invade. This creates a space for infection to grow, and we become our even-more-wounded self... yuck!

Turn inward! The silence is important. Trust that you will move in and out of this state—even as you work through this book. Pay attention to these unconscious responses. Bring them to consciousness and you may be pleasantly surprised how you can change your life by just being aware. The trance state (not paying attention) is a direct indication that you have your false-self on and your true-self off. It's your true-self that you need to see and hear if you're going to achieve an extraordinary life and balanced state of being.

Defining Your Set Point

Finally, it's important that you begin to develop a sense of what I call the "set point." It's really just a different way of looking at and sensing your balance, also known as emotional homeostasis. This is the point in the body where your core state is programmed, like a thermostat that measures the temperature of the environment and sets or adjusts your systems for optimum efficiency.

This place of origin is where you sense that you are on or off target. It's never pleasant when we receive the feeling that we are "off." When I started to work with this feeling it produced a stress response in my heart. You may experience it differently, but finding your set point challenges the status quo. That can create many sensations and responses, but you have to have some sense of your set point to find balance.

Think of it like the driver's seat of your essence. Your set point is different than the inner compass as it is the launching pad from where you can explore. The inner compass guides you when you leave the launching pad. Your set point calls you back home when you move too far from the launching pad.

Once you learn to recognize and interpret your set point, just imagine the possibilities! You will have the flexibility to explore new concepts and incorporate them into your daily life. With your set point established and stable, you will have the freedom to launch into new areas of your life with the security you need to really explore, knowing you can return to your place of balance easily and effortlessly. Think of it like a base camp that you're anchored to. You can go out and explore the region around you without fear. If you stray too far, it will pull on your tether and remind you to come back to "home base."

If your set point has been lost, it's not uncommon to have feelings of being lost. While you try to rediscover your set point, you may experience feelings of separation from your core. You may feel disconnected from the Universe and its infinite support. To regain the set point, you need to shift your focus from building your own self-esteem to focus instead on self-acceptance and an understanding that you are perfect just as you are.

This was a mind-blower for me. Once I accepted myself as I was, I found I could build from my core in a way that was unique and beautiful. It's like being a Christmas tree. If I am a Christmas tree, my job is not to build a tree, since that was already created perfectly by the Universe. I am to become the decorator of my tree.

I was created to be blessed in my life and I don't have to work on that piece of being "good enough" to be adorned. I am already somebody to be celebrated, just like everyone else in the world. And I don't have to work on "doing" my life and trying to build who I am through self-esteem work. I need to realize that accepting who I am allows me to focus my energy on more productive things, like ways I can bless my life and others.

Take a look around you. Do you see how the world is "doing" their life instead of allowing themselves to become what they were created to be? Watch out! Burnout is the symptom of just "doing" life and not becoming.

Growing and evolving is very important, but it's equally important to know that you come from a base of perfection. That means you accept all your flaws, mistakes and missteps as part of a greater plan. When you do this, you can move forward guided by your inner compass knowing that no matter what comes in your life, you are just being brought lessons and blessings and a richer understanding of your existence.

Discovery

I would like you to take some time now to do some self-work. Focus on your needs and wants and make two lists: one for your needs and one for the wants. Then make a list of each of these needs and wants divided into two categories: ones you have neglected and the ones in your life you are honoring. Put them side-by-side and weigh out how they have affected your balance.

Needs	Wants

Neglected	Honoring

You must remember that your life matters! Your needs and wants must be met to evolve to the next level of your life. If you don't fulfill your wants <u>and</u> desires and only focus on your needs, then you are merely maintaining. Focusing on wants and neglecting your needs leaves you susceptible to heartache and self-destruction because the solid foundation to support those wants is not there.

Think of this like a seesaw on a playground. It's a staple on many playgrounds because it's fun, but notice how quickly it loses its joy if everyone sits on one side. If you put too much weight on your needs, you lose fulfillment by not getting your wants met; if you put too much weight on your wants, you lose security and stability. By balancing both, you are able to not only survive but to thrive.

Tip: The key to success is to stay in balance, allowing your life source to flow naturally between needs and wants.

Wants   Set point   Needs

CHAPTER TWO

Integration of Our Navigation Systems

To effectively use your inner compass, you must take it a step further and connect your compass to your navigation systems. We are going to use the layers of the mind, our objective and subjective reality, and the duality of science and religion as our navigation systems. When you understand how to use your inner compass with your navigation system, you have the tools required to get safely to your true destination, even if you have never traveled this route before.

An accurate reading of the data is key. Even a slight misreading today can throw you way off course tomorrow.

The Layers of the Mind

There are three layers to the mind, the conscious, the subconscious, and the unconscious. In Freud's early work, he likened this to the ocean, with the exposed surface as the conscious, right below the surface of the water as the subconscious, and the depths of the ocean as the unconscious.

The conscious mind is your present awareness and what you are currently focusing on. It's the alert observer that gets signals from the five senses. It's the command center of the mind.

The subconscious mind is the part of your awareness that is not presently focusing, but can be easily recalled. This part of your mind holds a lot of your past experiences and memories that the brain stores until you are ready to access it again. An example would be the names of the people you know. When you see them or something that triggers a memory of them, you can easily recall those details (Okay, maybe not so easy for everybody!). Those details are quietly waiting just below the surface.

The unconscious is not conscious. They're the past experiences and memories that can influence you, but not on a conscious level. You are not aware of why you are triggered or reacting in a particular way. These are deeply stored memories that are usually only recalled through an intensely resonating trigger or event.

The three layers of the mind work together regularly. The conscious mind is the captain of the ship, making the decisions and delegating out the tasks for the day to the rest of the crew, the subconscious and unconscious mind. The captain holds the main responsibility for the ship, but the crew, with all of their wisdom and years of experiences, influence every action. If they stop interacting, the whole ship suffers either because nothing happens, or because the decisions are lacking information from the other crewmembers.

Objective vs. Subjective

You can see that we are each navigating our own ship in the same objective world, but our experiences and memories are what lead us to making subjective decisions based on our objective surroundings.

In psychological research, we consistently use quantitative (objective) and qualitative (subjective) data in our search for the truth. Science likes to place more value on the quantitative and much of the self-help world finds it more helpful to work with qualitative. Both are essential for complete understanding.

Have you ever had a friend who is really logical try to support you with a really emotional experience? Usually their logic is fairly on target, but the feeling of satisfaction and compassion is a bit disappointing. The opposite is also true. A friend that is really emotional might try to give you advice, saying something like "Dump him! He's a jerk! You deserve better!" This can feel impractical and impulsive since it lacks any reason behind it.

Objective and subjective inputs complement each other. One without the other just feels incomplete. Your observations hold truth, but your feelings do as well!

Science vs. Religion

Our world has been divided by science and religion. Some choose to navigate their life by the light of the most current, updated scientific research. Others use their religious beliefs as their guiding star.

From my therapeutic work, I've seen the value of both. I understand that expanding our knowledge through fact-based research into how the world really works can help my clients understand the mechanisms of biology and psychology and help prevent them from making the same mistakes time and time again. I've also seen how spiritual understanding has moved many of my clients through difficult situations that cannot be resolved by pure logic. Faith gave them the strength to move through the unknown.

The science world and the faith world made an agreement many years ago. At some point it was decided that science would focus on the physical world and faith would focus on the unseen. This created a clear but perhaps unnecessary divide between the two.

The detail that's often overlooked is that both approaches came from the same institutions of learning. The disciplines were just divided to avoid conflict and to create a non-threatening atmosphere for their studies. We may now think of them as mutually exclusive, but by bringing these two worlds together, we can have a more comprehensive understanding of the world we live in and discover a richer life experience.

We might use the term "cognitive dissonance" to describe this battle between science and religion. We hold in our minds two completely different explanations for the same phenomenon, but we learn from both.

I was raised with a primarily religious perspective. When I went back to school for my graduate programs, I was introduced to what seemed like a whole new world when I awakened my understanding of science. I was able to see how some of my belief systems were keeping me trapped, while other pieces of my belief systems were creating great resiliency and helping me thrive. When I integrated the scientific "facts of life" with deeply held spiritual principles, I found that life became more balanced and offered me a flexibility that was uniquely mine. By using both science and spirituality, I found a way to successfully navigate my internal and external world.

Integration

We are designed for the conscious mind and the subconscious mind to work together clearly and cohesively. This allows objective and subjective data to inform us in a richer way. We can call this melding action "integration" and it will allow us to extract ourselves from the pendulum of polar opposites.

Failure to integrate is like living with a split psyche, where we can see one perspective but have to leave it to see the other perspective. If we can't integrate, then we can't see the magic of the full spectrum. From my perspective, "I can't" isn't an option and integration is a must.

> *Wholeness is not achieved by cutting off a portion of one's being but by integration of the contraries.*
> *-Carl Jung*

The result is like letting a black and white TV come into full living color.

Creating cohesion between these vital components and consideration of the past, present, and future, allows us to assemble ourselves in such a way that is stronger, more flexible, and resilient. It reminds me of the Darwinian Theory of "survival of the fittest." You can come to be your best self by integrating all of your life experiences into a new form designed for optimal success.

> Tip:
> Notice "all or nothing" thinking and ask yourself "How could these different perspectives work together?"

CHAPTER THREE

The Integrated System

We've covered the basics, so now it's time for the deeper dive. Keep in mind the work you're getting ready to do is a move towards fulfillment. This is different than working on issues because you're "broken". Both are challenging, but one leads to success and the other leads to feelings of not being good enough.

As we move forward, we'll be covering seven areas that require our attention. These categories are areas of your life that, when fulfilled, lead you to a more satisfying and balanced life. These categories are as follows:

The Intellectual Body:
Belief Systems
Inner Knowing/Wise Mind
Perspectives
Knowledge from the Outside

The Spiritual Body:
Place of Truth
Integrity
Being Creative
Creating Your Dreams
Exploring the Unknown

The Emotional Body:
Healing Emotions
Transparency
Trapped Self
Energetic Walls
Spiritualizing Your Emotions

The Physical Body:
Physical Exercise
Eating and Drinking Right
Sleeping Well
Honoring Your Appearance
Honoring Your Time

Mastering Love:
Yourself and Others
Family/Partner
Community
Universe/Higher Power
Loving What Is

Zone Modifying:
Comfort Zones
Facing Your Fears
Letting Go of Control
Vulnerability
Boundaries

Integrating and Honoring the World Around You:
Home
Finances
Friends
Community
Earth and Its Creations
The World You Are In
A Hero

There are four "bodies" that one must consider as we navigate the concept of balance. Together they form the Holistic Body:

The Holistic Body consists of:
> The Intellectual Body
> The Spiritual Body
> The Emotional Body
> The Physical Body

The Intellectual Body

The mind is an amazing gift from the Universe. Its main purpose is to keep us safe and to act as a filtering agent, looking for ways to winnow out what hurts and keep in what is useful and safe. All the teachings from our lives are stored in this divine computer. The problem is that sometimes we have been taught things that don't serve our highest good.

We have to keep in mind that our teachings come from multiple sources: teachers, parents, media, music, etc. Not all their teachings are rooted in health. For example, if you had a parent that struggled financially they may have given you fear-based advice. "You have to save money so that you can always provide for your family," might be a common example of this kind of instruction. In some ways, this is an important message worth heeding, but can also be misread and taken out of context or too literally. You may end up thinking, "I shouldn't give myself what I want because family is more important than me." Family is important, but not more important than you. They are equally as important as you.

> "The root of all health is in the brain. The trunk of it is in the emotion. The branches and leaves are the body. The flower of health blooms when all parts work together."
>
> *Kurdish Saying*

Oftentimes, the mind holds on to the belief that it will stay safe if it will only allow safe experiences to transpire. This may limit the possible positive outcomes that could occur and limit reality to only opportunities that are defined by safety (i.e., no vacations, no extras, etc.). This will keep you living in the world of lack.

As we know from the law of attraction, you attract what you know, think or believe. If you believe in scarcity, you create scarcity; if you believe in abundance, you create abundance.

The Spiritual Body

The spiritual body is also known as the causative body. It has the highest vibrational frequency of all the energetic bodies. The spiritual body is the part of us that is immortal; the other bodies slowly dissolve over the course of time. The spiritual body is a gift that is too often overlooked. It is a place that needs to be acknowledged and nurtured so we can realize the highest essence of our self. We can be so afraid to take the time to sit with ourselves, to quiet the mind, to feel, or to dream. These actions are necessary to connect to the holistic body.

You may find it curious, as I have, that layers of emotions will continue to surface as you step more and more into the greatness of your spiritual self. Think of it like a flower going through the different stages of its growth. You too are a living, flowing being. New feelings will emerge throughout your life as you move into each level of your evolution. Painful experiences have divided us from our spiritual body and our journey is to move back toward it. We want the physical and spiritual to become one. The disconnection from our spiritual body is what causes our suffering. As we reconnect with our spiritual and higher selves, we will find our place of balance, and peace becomes the prominent emotion.

The Emotional Body

The emotional body is the place where our emotions are formed. We navigate the emotional world from our heart and our sensations. Feelings become the road signs of our lives and guide us to what steps we want to take next. As we become connected to multiple sources, such as our family, work, community, etc., we must master these connections to fully connect to our world in a healthy way.

When disconnected, we feel isolated and alone and we become misdirected. Our hearts close and we become miserable and detached from what we desire. Oftentimes we blame, project, judge, and avoid—all of which are attempts to repress what is oppressing us.

If we could allow the passing of the emotions, understanding that feelings are not who we are but something we are experiencing, we would quickly learn the power of emotions. We are the vessel to allow emotions to flow. When we accept this, we can see the transformation of our lives.

I want you to pay close attention to the perspective of the observer, the worrier, the critic, or the obsessed. These are all expressions of the separated self. Each will leave you feeling disconnected, afraid, and unworthy. Your true higher self is none of those things.

As you face your full range of emotions without restriction, you free the soul and move into a truer state. You allow the mind, body, spirit connection to work as one. This will allow you to finally flow as the natural being you were created to be.

The Physical Body

The physical body is the vessel that carries all of the other bodies. It is the one body that will cease to exist if not honored. All of the other bodies can function at some level without the other, but our productivity levels will be greatly decreased. The physical body is the direct messenger of truth. If you dishonor it, it will let you know. This is why it is so important to understand and honor that it is the guide that must be listened to if you want to master being in a state of balance.

I find it intriguing that we were given a physical shell to contain our greater selves. My understanding of it is that without limitations of the body, why would we stay? There is a reason we have been placed here on earth, but our desire to escape is so great at times that we were given the gift of containment. The body allows us to experience the human plane and allows us to stay grounded so that we don't leave.

This life was given to us to discover that who we are is as precious as the discovery of Universal love. We are all the same, but we have the opportunity to understand separation. This is what makes the desire for oneness more intriguing.

This also allows us to experience oneness because we all have a human body. No matter our differences, we are the same.

There is never a separation between our spiritual and our physical bodies, unless you don't honor either of them. You have to stand in both to understand the gift of the whole self.

If we were not in this body, we would not learn to stand in our own identity. We have to stand in our own light if we are to discover our true uniqueness.

Three Other Categories That Must Be Considered:

Integrating and Honoring the World Around You

Just as important as loving yourself is the act of loving things outside of yourself. A healthy love desires to give something to, rather than to always take something from. As we learn to value and respect the gifts of life, we gain great blessings and insights. See the beauty in all things, and as you do, you will see each holds a secret gift waiting to be a blessing for you.

Keep in mind some basic principles as you consider how you relate to the world around you:

- Let go of the idea that more is better. This pattern will leave you empty.
- See life as it is meant to be: a blessing, not a curse.
- Do not cling to anything. Nothing is permanent; holding on is just resisting life.
- Embrace what you have and be grateful for those gifts. They are resources!

Mastering Love

To be "in" love is to be in truth. Anything other than truth is separation from your true essence. When we separate from love we suffer through life because love is the fuel of our soul. What would happen if we could fully expand our heart and move back to a place of authentic love and connection? Why would you ever move back to the limited state of a closed heart again?

We must explore the world from a place of love, although many factors can get in the way of this, starting with fear, anger, loss, expectations, pain, and helplessness. These are all symptoms of disconnection from your heart.

Jungian theory in psychology suggests that the heart can be seen as two parts: the light and the shadow. The light is where love is natural and easy. The shadow is the place where love is lacking.

We desire to be in the light, but we often fall into the shadow. Both parts are necessary as they offer us an opportunity to expand our connection to the Universe through people, earth, and time. The shadow is a beautiful place for you to explore. The gifts inside are limitless and full of possibilities for you to feel the light of love. Think of it as a seed planted deep in the garden. The darkness and the dirt are as necessary as the sun to help the seed sprout and grow into a healthy plant.

The discomfort that comes from living only in the shadow creates the desire and drive to move back to the light. We use various "magical" techniques that we think will create a bridge from the shadow to the light. These might be sex, shopping, relationships, dancing, social events, or even isolation. These can all be useful and helpful tools, but when used incorrectly or as the *only* way, they can become addictions. Nothing limits us from standing in the light except for the belief that there is only one way. Our goal is to remember there are infinite ways!

Love is one of the greatest gifts we are offered, but many of us live our lives disconnected from it. We create conditions, excuses, and frustrations—more and more reasons why we can't have what is innate in all of us. **Love just is**.

You don't have to DO anything to get love. But because our primary care-givers—parents, friends, teachers, etc.—may have been incapable of giving us love at certain moments in our young lives, we come to believe that we can't ever get it without tricking, confusing, or outright manipulating someone to love us. This is where relationships can become exhausting, because you get tired of playing the "game."

Deciding to live in a world where no one can take away what you already have is nothing more than a miracle for the mind, body, and spirit. Always remember this truth and know that your love doesn't go away because someone you love leaves or is unable to meet your heart's desires. It's your gift and no one can take it away unless you believe it wasn't yours in the first place. That is an illusion in itself. **Love is.** No one owns it, so it can't be taken.

Zone Modifying

Through pain and suffering, we have been unconsciously trained to stay away from the gifts or doorways that would bring us to what our heart truly desires. We must go back towards the messages that these gifts contain. When we find the courage and strength to move toward these disconnected parts, we can once again reunite with our purpose.

Consider this example. Let's say you have someone in your life that you love with all your heart. You invest so much of yourself in this person that you began to lose you. The Universe, sensing the problem, throws you into a situation that forces you to explore the parts of you that you have devalued in order to feed the light of another. It points out the lack in you that makes you put this person on a pedestal. You're trying to solve something wrong in you by linking yourself to another person you sense has your missing strength.

Rather than connecting to someone because we feel inadequately equipped to navigate the world, we need to look back to our own feelings of inadequacy. They are trying to tell us something. And what do we learn? We are all equally valuable.

The Universe cannot tolerate the common distractions of our world and it will only allow us to lose our way for so long before it creates great discomfort – until it jostles our compass. I'm so grateful for this! The Universe is allowing us to navigate and experience the wonders of the unknown. It gives us feelings of security like love, safety, comfort, and support. When it sees you have stretched yourself to a place of harm, it will create tension, reminding you of the importance of coming home.

The Universe wants you to have everything you need and desire, but it wants to remind you that you may have been tricked into believing that to get it you must compromise yourself or others. That will not be tolerated and must be stopped before the gift can be received.

Throughout the book you will find charts to track your progress on this journey. Use the scoring guide to determine where you are in each category. I've included an example to show you how this might look.

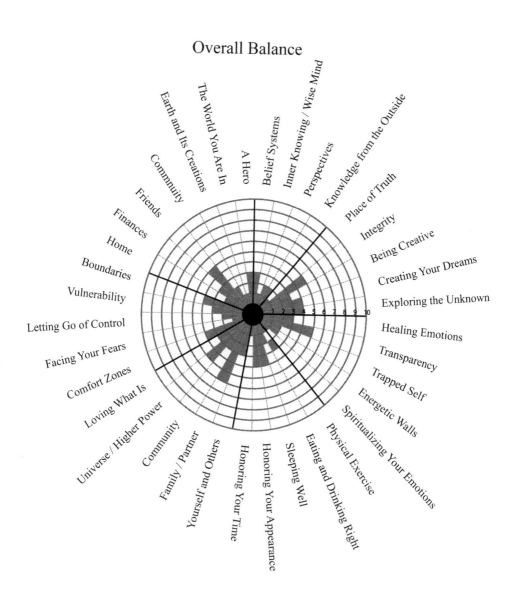

Overall Balance

Take an honest assessment of where you stand in these areas

Scoring guide:

1 = I realize there's a problem

2 = I have contemplated the issue

3 = I have considered actions steps for the issue

4 = I am prepared to take action

5 = I am taking necessary action steps

6 = I am taking action and I have already made some mistakes

7 = I am integrating lessons from failed action steps

8 = I am making adaptations to my actions

9 = I am being consistent in the actions needed

10 = I am at my ideal goal, I just need to maintain it

Overall Balance

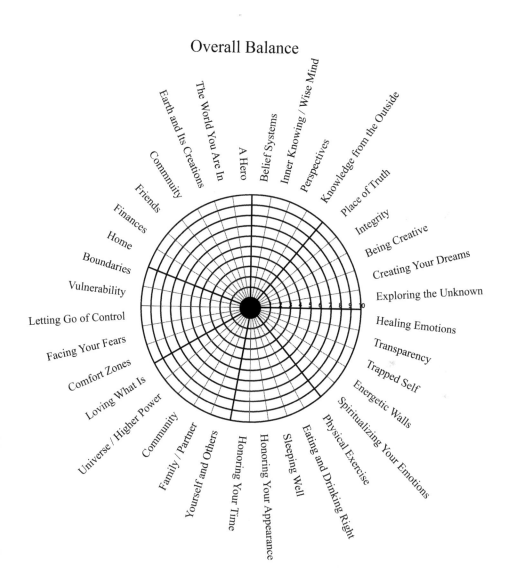

PART TWO

Exploring Balance

The second part of this book will be centered on exploring and shining love and light on the seven areas introduced in Part One. This will help you understand the value of restructuring these parts of your life, as well as show you how to expand on and explore them.

By taking these steps of developing a life that is based in love and truth, you will vibrationally re-align and shift what you attract. You engage the Law of Attraction, which is the idea that "like attracts like." You no longer attract what is out of balance, but that which is in balance. This is perfect synthesis; the inner and the outer are one.

A ship that is designed and built with materials that were made to handle extreme external forces is much more likely to stay afloat than one that is built quickly with only the lowest cost materials. The question is how have you built the ship of your life? Is it balanced and stable? Did you make strategic, wise choices or have you just done what was quick and easy? One will lead you to success; one will lead you to failure.

I want you to have the best life possible, so I bring this information to you so you can make the necessary adjustments to create the life you want. As we move forward, I will be explaining and guiding you through each category.

Each category is comprised of several elements. You can create balance in the category by working on the individual elements. I will define each element, show you how you can get out of balance in that element, and give advice about how to regain your balance. Then you will complete a self-assessment to select what elements you want to work on and to design personal strategies for working on each one.

It's going to make all the difference!

CHAPTER FOUR

The Intellectual Body

The intellectual body has its own range of feeling and expression. When there is too much focus within the limiting aspects of the mind, then thoughts become negative, full of judgment, fear, and depression. When thought expands into the more open-minded way of seeing the world, the mind can then see from the lens of compassionate-understanding, peace, joy, and happiness.

You will see that when you fill your mind with health it cannot help but start expanding into a greater world. Take the time to slow down and work on creating the kind of thoughts that generate the feelings you want. As you work through each of these categories, remember that every action creates a reaction. Let's get started.

Belief Systems

Much of the human race is attempting to operate on overdrive. We're all trying to "figure things out" or analyze what is safe and what is not. These are racing or pressured thoughts. Ultimately our goal is to use our mind in a more productive way. So rather than using it to manage the flow of your feelings so they don't overwhelm you, use your

"The more tranquil a man becomes, the greater is his success, his influence, his power for good. Calmness of mind is one of the beautiful jewels of wisdom."

James Allen

mind to make links and connections after the feelings have been fully expressed.

Dr. Jill Bolte Taylor, author of *A Stroke of Insight* found that the effect of trauma on the emotional body is approximately 90 seconds of emotional charge. However, the mind stretches the pain on and on for what can seem like an eternity.

I think of this like a balloon filled with air. If you pinch the opening so the air can only squeak out, it will take a long time to deflate. It will also hurt your ears and pretty soon your whole body will react to the obnoxious sound it emanates. You might be tempted to quit releasing the air and possibly even tie the end of the balloon into a knot, but that ends the process entirely.

In the same way, you might be tempted to stop healing because it brings up feelings that make you uncomfortable. You may even work very hard to avoid healing so you never have to feel again. We want to open our minds to pure potential, like a ship ready for its cargo. Just like a full container ship, if you compartmentalize and hold things in your body you're stuck. Without first unloading, there's no room for anything new. Let go of the old cargo to make room for the new.

Tip: High achieving people make more mistakes than low achieving people. If you can allow mistakes to happen and integrate the lessons, you will be headed in the direction of success.

To further awaken your mind, you should consider the following:

Stop:
- ✓ Searching for what is wrong.
- ✓ Comparing yourself to others.

✓ Questioning if you are missing something in you.
✓ Focusing on your pain. What you focus on, you create more of.
✓ Trying to understand why people think and behave the way they do.
✓ Trying to convince yourself that what you think is right.
✓ Testing your fears in your mind with endless "what ifs."
✓ Focusing on what you can't get.
✓ Judging others.

Start:
✓ Looking for what is right and continue to create more of it.
✓ Allowing the mind to go blank so wisdom can come through.
✓ Being open and anticipate what is coming. Get excited!
✓ Thinking of the beauty within and work on expressing it outwardly.
✓ Sending kind thoughts to the heart.
✓ Dreaming of what could be, rather than what you are used to.
✓ Being curious. Go out and explore the world. There is amazing work out there to be digested.
✓ Making connections between what you know and what you don't know.
✓ Reaching for new thoughts—ones that stretch you and make you question the thoughts you already have.
✓ Discerning what is in your highest and greatest good.
✓ Meditating.

Make a list of the areas you struggle with the most.
1.
2.
3.
4.
5.

What steps will you take to improve those areas?

1.

2.

3.

4.

5.

How will your life be different when you implement these changes?

_____

_____

_____

_____

_____

Tip: Challenge yourself to let go of beliefs and thoughts and see what comes.

Inner Knowing/Wise Mind

Your wise mind manifests itself when you allow internal wisdom to move through you. It moves first through the soul, then the spirit, and finally into the heart and mind. This is different than the traditional

Knowledge comes from the external world; wisdom comes from the inner world. To underestimate the value of either will leave you uneducated.

process of using your mind to gain knowledge and then adapting the internal aspects of your life accordingly. Inner knowing taps the wisdom you have already through a process of listening, trusting, and allowing until you have clarity.

This takes a lot of practice, patience, and a true desire to love yourself. If you have not been trained to go inward, this work will seem very difficult. You may want to consider finding a mental or spiritual counselor to help guide you through blocks that may be too difficult to overcome on your own. You may also find success by exploring meditation, self-help classes, journaling, or other self-honoring experiences that can help you tap into your inner wisdom.

Keep in mind that life happens in patterns. The most common pattern is circular. This is most obvious to us when we realize we've been repeating the same life choices over and over again. This also creates a self-fulfilling prophecy, since you predict the failure you already know is the result of the actions you keep repeating.

You can engage in a negative circular pattern that slowly erodes your life, or a positive one that supports you as you grow. You will see that putting others in front of you will lead to feelings of emptiness. If you put yourself before others, you will feel fulfilled and have excess to give to those you love.

Consider these two diagrams.

Self Fulfilling Prophecy
Others First - You Second

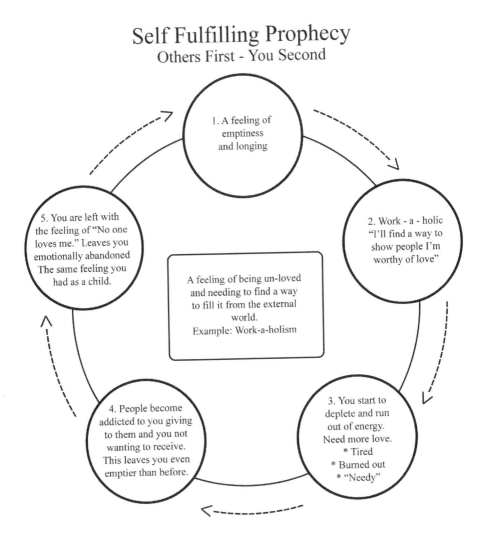

1. A feeling of emptiness and longing

2. Work - a - holic "I'll find a way to show people I'm worthy of love"

3. You start to deplete and run out of energy. Need more love.
* Tired
* Burned out
* "Needy"

4. People become addicted to you giving to them and you not wanting to receive. This leaves you even emptier than before.

5. You are left with the feeling of "No one loves me." Leaves you emotionally abandoned The same feeling you had as a child.

A feeling of being un-loved and needing to find a way to fill it from the external world.
Example: Work-a-holism

Shifting a Painful Loop
You First - Others Second

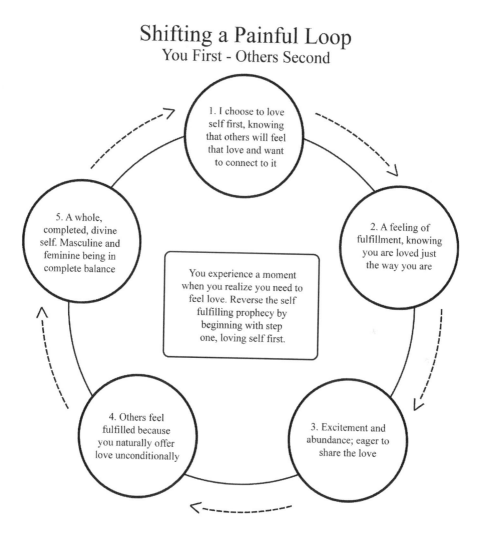

1. I choose to love self first, knowing that others will feel that love and want to connect to it

2. A feeling of fulfillment, knowing you are loved just the way you are

3. Excitement and abundance; eager to share the love

4. Others feel fulfilled because you naturally offer love unconditionally

5. A whole, completed, divine self. Masculine and feminine being in complete balance

You experience a moment when you realize you need to feel love. Reverse the self fulfilling prophecy by beginning with step one, loving self first.

Living from the inside out will help you develop an internal alarm system, one that will warn you if something is threatening you and will be at peace when you are safe. This creates a powerful sense of security, knowing that you are co-creating with the Universe and staying true to your core self.

If you seek knowledge from the outside world and attempt to bring it inward, it may conflict with who you are. It can create confusion, self-doubt, distortions, and eventually disconnect you from the Universe. Seek from within and allow the world to be illuminated by your inner knowing. Life will become so much easier and you won't need to live in self-doubt or wait for outside approval to feel good about yourself. That is a delicious gift.

To learn to make this shift, you must:

Stop:
- ✓ Distracting yourself from who you are.
- ✓ Avoiding going inward.
- ✓ Creating busy work to avoid your inner work.
- ✓ Putting others before yourself.
- ✓ Acting like you don't matter.
- ✓ Seeking knowledge rather than looking inward.
- ✓ Looking for someone else to confirm your worth. If someone chooses themselves, you will feel abandoned.
- ✓ Acting like you have no value. We all have value. When you act with value you will feel valued.
- ✓ Putting people on pedestals. That is your desire to be rescued. You must rescue yourself.
- ✓ Living in fear rather than faith. Fear creates more fear. Faith takes you out of trapped energy and moves you towards freedom.
- ✓ Acting dumb. You have something to share.
- ✓ Not trying because you don't want to feel your feelings. It's actually easier to grow when you try and then fail. Failure is feedback!
- ✓ Deferring to others who "know better." You are the only one who knows what is best for you.

Start:

✓ Sitting with yourself. It takes time and patience to reunite with the real you.

✓ Living as an equal to all things.

✓ Facing your fears, so they can transform into accomplishments.

✓ Understanding that what you admire in others is your own undiscovered gold.

✓ Examining old neglected parts of yourself.

✓ Looking at your enemies or those that annoy you to understand your shadow. They are the parts of you that you are rejecting. You can't heal until all parts are loved.

✓ Being patient and allow the Universe to show you the way to greatness.

✓ Asking others what they see you are avoiding.

✓ Being curious.

✓ Loving all of you, even the parts that you think are unlovable. All parts have a purpose.

Make a list of the areas you struggle with the most.

1.
2.
3.
4.
5.

What steps will you take to improve those areas?

1.
2.
3.
4.
5.

How will your life be different when you implement these changes?

_____

_____

_____

_____

_____

> Tip: Study great teachers and you will find your mind will be blown away by the work they have already done.

Perspectives

To grow, we must go out and search the world for new teachings. As you meet others with different interests and knowledge, you gain a greater perspective on the world and who you are. By comparing and contrasting what you've learned, you can stretch your worldview and allow your mind to expand in a way that will allow you to reach your highest potential.

Keep in mind the value of a limitless perspective—one that doesn't judge, but that honors all perspectives. I want you to see the world from a 360-degree view. This will allow your knowledge to be diverse and expansive. This is just as important as going inward. Looking at the inner world and the outer world both matter. You look within to discern your own truth about new ideas, but you find most of these new ideas by looking out. So you are working your mind in concert with your spirit. In this sense, the inner and the outer complement each other.

Want to get the most from your search for perspectives? Study things you wouldn't normally study. Look for new areas of interest and consider looking deeper into topics you discovered in the past. Through this process I know you will find there is more to you. You'll find you have a unique richness in your personality when you develop a deeper understanding of the world. As you learn your levels of capability will skyrocket.

After years of extensive education, meeting a diverse range of people, and traveling the world, the one thing I know for certain is that there is a lot of knowledge out there. The more I learn, the more there is to learn. Many gifts have surfaced in this process. It has opened my mind to infinite possibilities. I've found that there is no "one way." I've also found beauty from each lens, even heartache.

The goal is not to see through one lens, but to see through the lens of all.

By seeking out a greater perspective, we find there are infinite perspectives. That's when being stuck ceases to exist because there is always another lens to see through. The greater the perspective, the less stuck-ness. Do you see the gift in that?

To explore this further, you should:

Stop:
- ✓ Thinking that you know it all. There is always room for more wisdom.
- ✓ Judging and filtering information until there is nothing left to the message.
- ✓ Resisting differences. See the message and integrate it into a balanced place in your mind and heart. It should feel like love when this is done properly.
- ✓ Seeking knowledge from only one source. You may have a favorite, but keep listening to all sources to be open to new wisdom.
- ✓ Thinking knowledge only comes from the academic world. Friends, family, life experiences, and so much more can be your greatest teachers.
- ✓ Overlooking the wisdom in the moment. If you are in the future or the past, you just might miss a blessing in the now.
- ✓ Acting as if you "know." That stifles any growth and you cannot move beyond it.
- ✓ Pretending like you can't learn. We are all capable of learning new things. Try!
- ✓ Saying you will get to it, but you need life to slow down.

✓ Avoiding growth.

Start:
✓ Seeking new teachings.
✓ Getting excited about new ways of thinking.
✓ Looking for information that makes you curious.
✓ Looking where you have never looked before.
✓ Trusting your ability to learn. Once you get the wheels turning you will be surprised how quickly you will pick it up.
✓ Dreaming of what you want to be and get moving. Create!
✓ Examining history and how the world has found its way to where we are now.
✓ Looking at what others are learning and loving.
✓ Examining information you disagree with. Does it affect your shadow? Does it throw your way of viewing the world off?
✓ Opening your mind.
✓ Asking questions and stretching your mind.

Make a list of the areas you struggle with the most.
1.
2.
3.
4.
5.

What steps will you take to improve those areas?
1.
2.
3.
4.
5.

How will your life be different when you implement these changes?

_____

_____

_____
_____
_____

Tip: Find one thing
that you have wanted
to learn about and learn
what others have done to
obtain knowledge in
that field of study.

Knowledge from the Outside

There is so much to learn and know in the world. Other teachers have already eagerly explored and presented their knowledge for you. All you have to do is get out there and find it. Use the public library, the Internet, school, or whatever way is best for you; just do it! It is important for us to research and find our own meanings and understandings of these teachings. Stretch your mind by grappling with others' work.

You don't have to know everything and the beauty of this is that others have been blessed with the resources they needed to go find the information for you. Now you need to immerse yourself in that knowledge. Find teachings that evoke emotion and engagement. They will allow you to expand.

Find balance in your work as well as others. Know that both are necessary for the perfect expression of you. Always stretch yourself in the search for new knowledge. You won't regret it.

I have loved the process of learning and will never stop this quest for knowledge. I make a list of areas I want to study and explore. Then I look for trainings and teachings in those areas. This feeds me just as much as play.

So many clients come into my office with this core issue of needing more knowledge but are seemingly unconscious of this need. They complain that something is missing in their life, there's no time, no money, and they've run out of ideas of what to do. That's my red flag. It's a direct sign that they have run empty and that they're ready for a refill. The next step is to simply ask, "Have you thought about pursuing more education, exploring new concepts, or taking some classes?"

> *The knowledge in the world holds keys to the internal world. Utilize these keys to unlock your potential.*

In our twenty first century world of the Internet and public education, it's easy to explore, research, and integrate new ideas into our greater wellbeing. Knowledge is the fertilizer for your seed. It's here to help you grow in a bigger and more beautiful every day. If you starve yourself of this fertilizer, you may still grow, but not to your full potential.

To develop this area for yourself, try the following:

Stop:
- ✓ Avoiding school, reading, and knowledge.
- ✓ Thinking there is one truth. There are unlimited beliefs and each will lead you down different roads. Explore them and find what is right for you.
- ✓ Ignoring the things that don't interest you. Sometimes there are hidden gifts in the areas you reject.
- ✓ Saying "I can't" or "I'm dumb." That is just a trick you are playing on yourself.
- ✓ Believing you are incapable of learning. This is just fear. Everyone is capable of learning and expanding. Do it at your own pace.
- ✓ Believing something is too hard. One step at a time and everything can become manageable.
- ✓ Believing anything is outside of your scope of possibilities. There are no glass ceilings, just the illusion of self-imposed ones.
- ✓ Distracting yourself with too much screen time and useless information that doesn't help you grow.
- ✓ Wasting time avoiding ideas.
- ✓ Doing only what you can do instead of working on what you can't.

Start:

- ✓ Looking for like minds. Surround yourself with people who want to learn and grow just like you.
- ✓ Trusting your curiosity. It will lead you to just the right information.
- ✓ Looking for teachers you resonate with. You always want a team of experts around you.
- ✓ Making a list of areas you want to know more about.
- ✓ Asking others what they love. Learn from their stories and teachings. Everyone has something to teach.
- ✓ Studying those who have accomplished your dreams. They may be showing you the path to walk.
- ✓ Studying at your developmental level. Trust things will make sense if you look for what is easy. You can get more complex as you learn.
- ✓ Trusting the process of going from small concepts to big ones.
- ✓ Getting curious about what you don't know.

Make a list of the areas you struggle with the most.

1.
2.
3.
4.
5.

What steps will you take to improve those areas?

1.
2.
3.
4.
5.

How will your life be different when you implement these changes?

_____

_____

_____

_____

_____

Take an honest assessment of where you stand in these areas

Scoring guide:

1 = I realize there's a problem

2 = I have contemplated the issue

3 = I have considered actions steps for the issue

4 = I am prepared to take action

5 = I am taking necessary action steps

6 = I am taking action and I have already made some mistakes

7 = I am integrating lessons from failed action steps

8 = I am making adaptations to my actions

9 = I am being consistent in the actions needed

10 = I am at my ideal goal, I just need to maintain it

The Intellectual Body

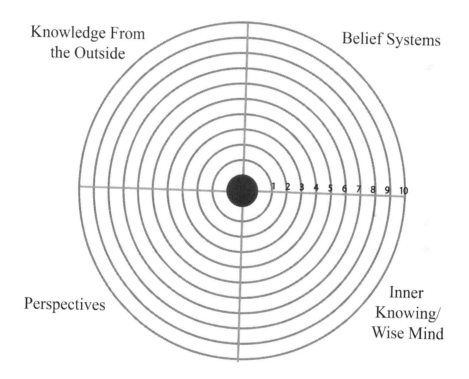

Knowledge From
the Outside

Belief Systems

Perspectives

Inner
Knowing/
Wise Mind

1 2 3 4 5 6 7 8 9 10

CHAPTER FIVE

The Spiritual Body

The spiritual body is the energy that is contained within the physical body. It holds all the ingredients that make up who you are. This energy forms its own being and expresses itself in many familiar ways including love, emotions, urges, and desires.

The spiritual body is such a beautiful expression of our higher self. Gaining and working with this connection can be powerful beyond measure, but in our society, very little effort is made to explore this body. I think this is because we've become very literal in our understanding of life. If we can't see it, it isn't real. In my practice, I find that kind of misunderstanding is often linked to individuals are struggling to know their purpose.

When a dear friend of mine was asked, "What do you want to do with your life?" she would always answer, "I don't know! I'm a Jack-of-all-trades. I can't find my purpose." I can confirm, from personal observation, that this was true. She was an incredibly capable woman, who could do just about anything and could figure almost everything out. She was the type that could skim through a complex set of directions and then, basically, just figure out the project on her own. But she couldn't see how that revealed her purpose.

I always knew she was more than just a generalist, or a Jack-of-all-trades. There was something special about her ability to integrate information and put it into practical form. Yet she would discount her ability as if it had no value and certainly didn't allow it to express her purpose in the world.

As I watched her develop over many years, I could see that she truly had a great gift. Her only error was that she was not aware of what it was. She was acting it out, daily! She helped integrate and simplify concepts for individuals. She learned to work with the earth and animals, and eventually taught people how to connect with earth medicine, and the messages of simplicity and truly being present.

Only recently has she started to recognize that what she was doing all along was her greatest gift to the world. Her unconscious rejection of who she was, was the only thing that separated her from recognizing her purpose.

To live out your life in a purposeful way is what creates your purpose. When you are searching for your purpose before acting, that's what keeps it hidden. What you love and what you are <u>is</u> your purpose.

Purpose is a spiritual connection.

Place of Truth

There is wisdom you hold within. If you will let it, this internal "knowing" will percolate up to the surface. You have to believe that it has a greater meaning in the world and that you are the channel of this information. Take time to meditate, release distractions, and become curious about your unfolding truths.

At times you will feel no call to the well within. At other times you will wake up to it screaming and begging you to express it! This takes a lot of patience as well as kind and loving thoughts of faith. You must

> *Truth for one man may not be truth for another. Value all truths and the battle of lies will be over.*

trust that we all have wisdom and a purpose for expressing it. You are the only one who is meant to convey your wisdom from within

Be patient with yourself. Trust that you have great value in this world. Take the time to be with those feelings and know that they can be uncomfortable at first. As you learn to work with them and bring them to the surface it will get easier and easier.

I remember when I started working on this book. I was so afraid! I thought I was a well of emptiness. Surely, I had nothing that the world would ever want to hear. Now I know that what I hold inside is meant for others. It's also a blessing for me to see my own growth.

I want this for you. I want you to see the value of what is inside you. If you skip this step, you will consistently seek others to confirm you are enough. I want you to see your internal bounty, and the only way to gain this treasure is to go on a quest to find it, like the explorers who mapped the globe.

When you find it, and you will, share it with the world and stand in the blessing of knowing you are leaving a legacy!

> Tip:
> Trust the process and listen. This takes practice and a quiet mind. Going into nature can help with this process.

To grow in this area, you should consider the following:

Stop:
- ✓ Thinking you have nothing to give to the world. Everyone has something to contribute.
- ✓ Making excuses that you have no time. Make time and build it into your schedule.
- ✓ Distracting yourself. No one creates from a distracted mind.
- ✓ Comparing to others' work. Your work is yours. No one else will ever compare to the original.
- ✓ Thinking you aren't good enough. The only way you ever feel your best is to take the first step, and then another, and another.
- ✓ Trying to make it perfect. Trust that, as it is created, you can adjust it.

✓ Saying it is too big or too small. Don't define the outcome. Let it be as it's meant to be.
✓ Taking too much on so you can't do the work. Create a balanced workload so you can have space in your life to create.
✓ Playing your abilities down. Just try. I promise it's in there.

Start:
✓ Creating, period! Use the Law of Inertia. An object at rest will remain at rest unless acted upon by another force. An object in motion continues in motion (so stay in motion).
✓ Trusting the process. It will unfold.
✓ Clearing distractions and make a space for projects to get completed.
✓ Meditating and being with your feelings. Listen for inspiration.
✓ Knowing that boredom is a call to the well of creativity.
✓ Moving towards the places that scare you as those are the places where the gift is.
✓ Listening to the small voice within and working with it. Make sure you are listening to your higher self and not that pesky ego. Ego is loud and judgmental; the higher self is quiet and comes from a place of love.
✓ Looking at your deepest issues in life; at your core. That's likely where the gifts lie.
✓ Sitting still.

Make a list of the areas you struggle with the most.
1.
2.
3.
4.
5.

What steps will you take to improve those areas?
1.
2.
3.

4.

5.

How will your life be different when you implement these changes?

_____

_____

_____

_____

_____

<u>Integrity</u>

If I could teach you just one value that has made a significant impact in my life, it would be to stand in integrity. Integrity is being true to your heart and doing the best you can to honor others' hearts. It's making your best attempt to do the "right thing" in all circumstances, no matter if you are being watched or not. This can take incredible courage and strength and will take a lot of effort. It is <u>so</u> worth it, though.

In the past I really struggled with this. I had some negative behaviors that weren't very pretty. I was afraid of being exposed and that fear grew over time. I worried that these behaviors weren't lovable and I felt ashamed. All I wanted to do was hide.

As I got older the feelings of incongruence grew. I felt like I was splitting in two from the inside out. My anxiety went up and I knew I had to make a change. I wept as my world crashed around me, but I made a commitment to be in 100% integrity. Oh boy! The Universe had plans for me and the next seven years of my life were affected in a profound way.

There is an incredible payoff for making this commitment. It was not easy, but I will tell you this: the anxiety was gone. I felt strong and I felt like I had

> *Integrity is to be true to the heart, and by doing so your light shines the way for others.*

nothing to lose. I was being true to my life and doing the best I could to honor others. I felt like I had value by just being me.

I can't say I've hit the 100% mark yet, but I feel so much better now that I know I am on the right track! If integrity is the path you choose to walk, you let life flow through you without any roadblocks. You are efficient, pure and true. You return to the true essence of what you were created for.

Make a list of areas in your life you know are incongruent with integrity. Each day, be conscious of these inconsistencies and make an effort to realign yourself. One day, just as I did, you will turn around and be very proud of your life. You will be at peace, knowing you are in complete union with your essence.

> Integrity feels right, no guilt, and no remorse. It may be hard, but you will feel strong and true in your core.

To explore integrity, take these steps:

Stop:
- ✓ Criticizing others for actions you have taken.
- ✓ Putting on a false persona.
- ✓ Manipulating others.
- ✓ Devaluing.
- ✓ Cheating, lying, or stealing.
- ✓ Condoning unethical behaviors.
- ✓ Intentionally misrepresenting information.
- ✓ Vilifying others to make yourself look good.
- ✓ Acting immorally or condoning the immoral acts of others.
- ✓ Bullying others or ruling by intimidation and threats.
- ✓ Embarrassing or humiliating people who work for and with you.

✓ Doing something that you would be ashamed to tell to your mother or children.
✓ Acting for selfish gain.
✓ Projecting.

Start:
✓ Being consistent in your actions.
✓ Encouraging and affirming others.
✓ Walking your own talk.
✓ Valuing others' opinions.
✓ Keeping your word.
✓ Being honest and forthright, even when it's hard.
✓ Being of good character.
✓ Being a positive example and role model.
✓ Being principled in your actions and stand up for what you believe.
✓ Behaving ethically.
✓ Considering others.
✓ Being loyal in a way that helps others feel safe.
✓ Being fair.

Make a list of the areas you struggle with the most.
1.
2.
3.
4.
5.

What steps will you take to improve those areas?
1.
2.
3.
4.
5.

How will your life be different when you implement these changes?

_____

_____

_____

_____

_____

Being Creative

We are all seeds, here to create a unique expression of ourselves. If we won't allow this to occur, we are just being templates or copies of others. You will feel a hunger within, begging you to allow the expression of you – and it will keep nagging you until you do. This stage in the process of balance is so important. Making space for our creative flow is how we step into who we are.

Now this doesn't necessarily mean you will suddenly paint, draw, or sculpt. But the arts aren't the only ways to express creativity. It may mean you will speak, touch a life in a unique way, or be known for something that is exclusive to you. I don't know what that is for you, but I do know you need to find what it is in order to feel fulfilled.

When I withheld these seeds from the world, I became disenchanted, angry and bitter – all projections of my own self-hate. Turn these into signs you need to be creative.

Carl Jung stated, "If you do not use your shadow, your shadow will use you." Your shadow holds repressed pain and gifts, which may be your seeds for future legacies and your higher self. If you find yourself bored, it's usually a direct indication that you need to be creative.

Create beyond the mind and you will allow your internal passion to color your external world.

I remember going through a phase where I was feeling very bored and I found myself irritated with everything in the world. My honey was on Facebook and the TV was on and everyone was paying attention to something other than me. I was very irritated about it all.

I found my inner child screaming for attention and I wanted to micro-manage every nuance of these annoyances. Then I realized that there might be—there MUST be—a better way, but I wasn't quite sure how to manifest it.

My first inclination was to pull away from my partner, to show her what a mistake she was making by focusing on Facebook and not me. I wanted to project all my thoughts about why she was a terrible person and make it known I was being greatly neglected. Then I realized that these thoughts were not leading me to great places, nor were they helping my relationship. I needed to find a more practical way to transform this energy in my body.

Then I remembered something I read on a card somewhere, a basic principle: **spiritual boredom is a call to be creative**. What a concept! You mean this time that I am sitting here masterminding my revenge on an evil world was not correct?! Hmmm! What could I do with this energy?

I went on a quest to create and that was the beginning of my writing career. Now, every time I start to sense those feelings of boredom, I know it's the call to develop a new product, find new inspiration, or create a gift from my soul to the world. Almost immediately, the energy starts to pour out.

If your sailing becomes mundane, drop anchor, put on your wetsuit, and dive in to find your treasure!

Tip:
Sit down and pull some supplies together. It may be a pad of paper, pencils, a tape recorder or whatever your creative side feels it is meant to express. Have no agenda, and let a creation emerge. Just see what happens.

To enhance creativity in your life, consider the following:

Stop:
- ✓ Saying there is nothing special about you.
- ✓ Believing you aren't creative.
- ✓ Focusing on things that zone you out like Facebook, TV, video games, or other people's problems.
- ✓ Thinking about what you can't do.
- ✓ Saying "I'm bored."
- ✓ Doubting that there is more.
- ✓ Always doing the same thing you did the day before.
- ✓ Criticizing yourself.
- ✓ Being a perfectionist.
- ✓ Focusing on what you can't do, rather than what you can.
- ✓ Stealing from your precious gifts or using them in a way that is wasteful or neglectful (e.g., creating lies, stories, gossiping).

Start:
- ✓ Taking time to tune into what you love.
- ✓ Doing something creative.
- ✓ Allowing the energy in your body to build
- ✓ Going into nature. This brings you back to your source.
- ✓ Nurturing your craft.
- ✓ Putting yourself and your creative gifts into the world without trying to gain approval.
- ✓ Leaving your legacy.
- ✓ Doing what you can do and trusting it will grow as you work with its energy.
- ✓ Playing with different ideas.
- ✓ Trying new things.
- ✓ Getting to know others who are creating.
- ✓ Moving towards creative opportunities like fairs or shows, etc.

Make a list of the areas you struggle with the most.

1.

2.

3.

4.

5.

What steps will you take to improve those areas?

1.

2.

3.

4.

5.

How will your life be different when you implement these changes?

_____

_____

_____

_____

_____

Creating Your Dreams

Once you've unleashed your creativity you will reach the point when it's time to take this new creative aspect of yourself to the next level. You'll feel the need to go from what might be called "simple" creativity (drawing, crafting, writing) to a kind of creativity that makes dreams come true. When you reach this point, you'll be making something that will become your legacy.

This personal legacy will allow you to know that you are enough, no matter what the world says, because you will be following your own path rather than what the world dictates for you. It feels fantastic to follow your own path rather than to follow the programming of someone else's path.

This book is one of my many dreams. I wrote this book not for social approval or for validation of who I am, but as an expression of love. I have something important within me that needs to be shared. If my book is a success and others learn from it, then that will be icing on the cake. But the opportunity to get this message out is the core of what drives me. I have many seeds ready to become a harvest and I will spend the rest of my life bringing them into physical form.

> *Faith with action is the doorway to success. If you believe it, you can create it.*

What if Thomas Edison or Martin Luther King didn't bring their dreams to the world? What a loss that would be. Can we really afford to not do what we were designed to do?

Tip:
Start with a project and release any need for approval, either at the beginning or the end of the project. When it's completed, give it to the world as a gift and trust that the seed will be received as it is meant to be. This may be a book, a class, art, blog, or even something you built, etc.

Consider the following:

Stop:
- ✓ Waiting for approval.
- ✓ People pleasing.
- ✓ Getting caught up in other people's business.
- ✓ Using excuses.
- ✓ Underestimating yourself.
- ✓ Telling yourself no.
- ✓ Getting caught up in your emotions.
- ✓ Letting the excuses of your life be a priority over your purpose.
- ✓ Doing anything that does not follow your heart.
- ✓ Being afraid. You were made to do this.
- ✓ Comparing yourself to others.
- ✓ Being a perfectionist.
- ✓ Thinking you are the message. You are the messenger.
- ✓ Thinking it is too much responsibility.

Start:
- ✓ Making a life you are proud of.
- ✓ Stretching yourself out of your comfort zones on a regular basis.
- ✓ Integrating failures into opportunities to strengthen your will.
- ✓ Taking life challenges as tests towards flexibility.
- ✓ Allowing each and every interaction to feed you through the experience.
- ✓ Looking for the gifts in the moment.
- ✓ Letting go of the old you and letting in the new you.
- ✓ Embodying your essence and letting all your bodies start to work together.
- ✓ Being excited about opportunities.
- ✓ Enjoying finding out what your purpose is rather than needing to say what it is.
- ✓ Getting incredibly curious about anything that wakes you up. That's how you know you are on the right path.

Make a list of the areas you struggle with the most.

1.
2.
3.
4.
5.

What steps will you take to improve those areas?

1.
2.
3.
4.
5.

How will your life be different when you implement these changes?

_____

_____

_____

_____

_____

Exploring the Unknown

The unknown is typically something we can't control. This elicits tremendous fear, so we cope by focusing on anything else. We might actually shift our attention to dwell on things like old wounds, our relationships, and our weaknesses. The past becomes the focus of our thought, primarily because it is known.

The funny thing is, you have to move into the unknown to grow. We used to think the world was flat and feared we would sail off the face of the Earth, but through exploration we realized that fear was unfounded. What a mind-trip!

Fear of the unknown is why we keep recreating past wounds and projecting them into our future. To move forward, we need to let go of our old ideas and belief systems and take a risk. Trust that you have the tools and resources now to move forward with success.

I remember actually saying "Well, I just know," as if this were some kind of prophesy or statement and that there was no other way. What an illusion! There is my way and a billion-zillion other ways as well. Saying "I know" is my way of saying all the other ways are too scary and I don't want to know. The need to be all-knowing is really just a core fear of exploring.

> *Never be afraid of what you don't know, get excited for what's coming!*

I remember a time in my life when I was stepping into the world of metaphysics, despite coming from a conservative, Baptist upbringing. The unknown felt like a black abyss in many ways, because I was taught to believe that this was dangerous territory where darkness loomed. The feelings of righteousness that came from that perspective gave me a false sense of being in control.

As I released that shell of protection and stepped into the unknown, the world I thought I knew started to unravel before me. I found my connection to a higher power take on new and different forms, though I never lost the belief that it was there loving me, supporting me.

This was confusing, because my old beliefs said that I was stepping out from under the hedge of protection. "You're on your own, Lisa. You'll face the dark dragons of the underworld alone!" I'll tell you a secret. I faced that dragon, but instead of hurting me, that dragon brought me magic, higher wisdom, and a deeper relationship to my higher power.

There are other gifts that I found by exploring this new world that surpass my ability to document in this book, but it's safe to say it woke me up to the infinite gifts of the Universe's potential. Love, as well as pain, moves beyond belief, and can touch the lives of all.

No matter what world you are in, love exists. When you realize this gift, you can move forward fearlessly, knowing that the illusion of "one way" actually strips you of the power of continuing on. You, too, must explore other worlds to truly be a part of the adventure.

Truth is in the heart. If something is right for you, move forward without over-analyzing it or trying to convince anyone else why you are right or by "making a point." Follow your heart and let your life reflect truth.

Tip: Take one fear on and write down step by step how your perception changes as you face that fear. Notice when it is completed how it links to your higher purpose, and how you want to love better than you have before the fear was addressed.

To develop in this area, consider the following:

Stop:
- ✓ Trying to figure out what the unknown looks like.
- ✓ Figuring out ways to navigate around the future.
- ✓ Trying to control other people and situations.
- ✓ Focusing on problems.
- ✓ Clinging to ideas of how it should be.
- ✓ Focusing on your fears.
- ✓ Needing to over-plan.
- ✓ Creating distractions.
- ✓ Saying you can't.
- ✓ Clinging to what you know.
- ✓ Saying "I need to understand it before I can do it or move forward."
- ✓ Starting every thought with "what if…"
- ✓ Worrying.
- ✓ Thinking so much.
- ✓ Presupposing what the outcome will be.

Start:
- ✓ Letting go of needing to know.
- ✓ Opening your heart and embracing the moment.
- ✓ Having faith that the resources you need will be there.
- ✓ Taking appropriate risks.
- ✓ Looking for what is right.
- ✓ Breathing into the fear and being present with it so it can dissipate.
- ✓ Getting curious about what could be coming.
- ✓ Going with the flow of life.
- ✓ Enjoying the experience.
- ✓ Taking action rather than thinking.
- ✓ Sitting with the feeling of not knowing.
- ✓ Meditating.

Make a list of the areas you struggle with the most.
1.
2.
3.
4.
5.

What steps will you take to improve those areas?
1.
2.
3.
4.
5.

How will your life be different when you implement these changes?

_____

_____

_____

_____

_____

Take an honest assessment of where you stand in these areas

Scoring guide:

1 = I realize there's a problem

2 = I have contemplated the issue

3 = I have considered actions steps for the issue

4 = I am prepared to take action

5 = I am taking necessary action steps

6 = I am taking action and I have already made some mistakes

7 = I am integrating lessons from failed action steps

8 = I am making adaptations to my actions

9 = I am being consistent in the actions needed

10 = I am at my ideal goal, I just need to maintain it

Spiritual Body

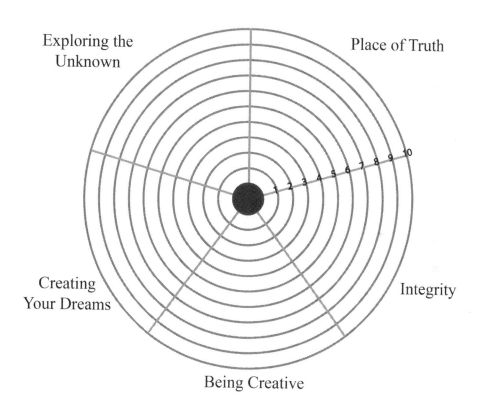

Exploring the Unknown

Place of Truth

Creating Your Dreams

Integrity

Being Creative

CHAPTER SIX

The Emotional Body

The emotional body is such a blessing because it is really what keeps us growing and evolving on our path. Through experiencing the full range of emotions, we are able to illuminate the messages of our unconscious, subconscious, and conscious needs. With a little practice, we can feel what serves us and what doesn't and make positive steps forward in our lives.

If someone has numbed out or disconnected from these messages they will struggle to know how to navigate their path. I want you to be in charge of your life. You deserve great things! You need to be true to yourself to create greatness in your life.

"The secret of health for both mind and body is not to mourn for the past, not to worry about the future, or not to anticipate troubles, but to live the present moment wisely and earnestly."

Siddhartha Gautama Buddha

Healing Emotions

Emotions are the buoys in our lives. If you have struggled with emotions, you may find yourself becoming moody at unexpected times or without warning. The emotions may seem out of place or out of context. This is a state where multiple emotions are surging through your body, but you can no longer connect them to the trigger or the reason for the emotion. You need to slow down, tune in, and honor how your emotions are trying to guide you.

Keep in mind that emotions are like water moving through a pipe. The body is that pipe. You must let the emotional fluid flow through the body without restricting or blocking the flow, then the greatest things in life are possible. Doesn't that sound fantastic? Imagine a life that gives you the best possible results.

Family patterns can play a big role in how you manage emotions. Keep in mind that if your family doesn't know how to express emotions in a healthy way, you probably won't either. Find others who can support you as you learn new ways to emote.

In family-of-origin work, we find that many of our life behavior patterns come from what we have observed from our primary caregivers. The gift in our observations is discovered when they model a healthy life that is in balance. That shows us how to build a life that is useful and desirable.

However, if your family of origin model life patterns that lead to addiction, sex abuse, or poverty, it's useful to shift away from these aspects of your life in order to create a place of safety and to re-learn core concepts that can lead you to higher ground. In essence, we can use them as an example of what not to do. That's still a valuable gift.

So, if your navigational system has been pre-programmed to go too close to shore, unless you know this and are willing to embrace the necessary changes, you'll find your ship damaged and possibly sinking. To avoid this, you may need to pause in the middle of the ocean to recalculate your course and reprogram your systems.

Recalculation might require a bit of time and thinking. That's ok; it's worth it! Start by asking yourself some basic questions like:

- What do I hope to accomplish?
- What do I need to be successful?
- Where are my vulnerabilities?
- What are my needs?

By doing some self-awareness work and answering good questions, you become conscious and emotional at the same time, which allows you to protect yourself, while also acknowledging the need to let go. It's almost like you're taking the role of parent <u>and</u> child and allowing both to have a voice.

> Tip: Quiet yourself and just let your emotions be, without labeling them or trying to wrap a story around them. Breathe into what you are feeling and express them completely. Sometimes even giving a sound like a moan or a physical movement like rocking can help.

To develop your emotional body, explore the following:

Stop:
- ✓ Denying your pain.
- ✓ Judging your emotions.
- ✓ Acting like your emotions are not important. They are telling you something. Feel them. Observe them. Listen to their literal and subtle messages.
- ✓ Avoiding your emotions. Go toward them.
- ✓ Making your emotions other people's issues. They are your responsibility.
- ✓ Believing that your emotions are you. Emotions are separate from the person. They do not define who you are. They are the road signs of life. Use them as that.
- ✓ Clinging to your emotions. They are meant to pass through you. Clinging is a fear response.

✓ Being afraid of your emotions. We are meant to work with them, not to feel like they control us.

✓ Associating your emotions to the idea that "something is wrong." Emotions are just signs. Use them to guide you on your path.

✓ Chasing your emotions. If they are meant to be felt, they will be there. Chasing them can make them run away.

✓ Trying to create your emotions. Stop making up stories in your head to create the sensation of feeling loved or hurt, etc. Created emotions can manifest into an addiction of control.

✓ Putting a story around them. The story, more often than not, is what holds them in place. Release the story; release the pain.

✓ Needing to "know" them. Needing to know your emotions stops you from expanding past what you know. Outgrow your past.

✓ Escaping them all together. How can you move towards wholeness if you won't embrace all of the expressions of you?

✓ Labeling your emotions. Just be with them. That's what feelings are: a cognitive expression of what you think emotions are.

Start:
✓ Being curious about your emotions. Curiosity stirs up the essence of what and who you are.

✓ Understanding that they are the door to freedom.

✓ Observing them without judgment. Love them and help them pass.

✓ Being kind to them.

✓ Going towards them and seeing what they want from you. Release them so you can see what they want to give you like messages, healing, etc.

✓ Nurturing them and encouraging them to rise to the surface.

✓ Touching your body where you feel them. Send a loving intention and ask them to communicate with you.

✓ Breathing into them. Conscious breath allows emotions to move through you with less effort.

✓ Sending love and light to your emotions.

✓ Talking about them to people who can listen for wounds and thinking errors.
✓ Playing and feeling positive emotions, as well as the hard ones.
✓ Embracing your pain as part of life.
✓ Making space for a new reality and emotional growth.

Make a list of the areas you struggle with the most.
1.
2.
3.
4.
5.

What steps will you take to improve those areas?
1.
2.
3.
4.
5.

How will your life be different when you implement these changes?

_____
_____
_____
_____
_____

Transparency

Expressing yourself is key to the success of your evolution. And when I say "express yourself" I mean for you to shine out your full energy without attempting to mask or change who you are for the approval of others.

Think of the 1939 movie "The Wizard of Oz." Oscar Zoroaster Diggs, the Kansas conman, masked himself as "Oz, the Great and Terrible," who was all-powerful and could do anything. In reality, he was secretly terrified by knowing that he couldn't really do anything. He was just a man who was lost on his adventure, a fact he clearly didn't want anyone else to know. So, when pressed, he would put on a dramatic show of fire and smoke to distract the people. Impressed, they would work hard to please him. Then he could control the situation and dispense his approvals.

I think we can all relate to this on some level. We don't want the world to know that we don't really know what to do. So we hide behind our personas, hoping no one will look behind the curtain and see that we are desperately trying to hold everything together.

Don't mask yourself. Don't present yourself as something you're not. You're too precious for that! This is where relationships, careers, finances, and so many other areas can go south. If you put all your energy into making life look one way, I promise you, you will forget all the other ways.

> *Transparency is magic, if you have it you can walk through barriers.*

Allow all the pieces of you to shine. No matter how good or bad they make you look. There is an incredible peace that will come to your life if you can just allow yourself to be authentic, with no need to adjust who you are when others see you. Step out from behind the curtain and realize that your humanness is what makes you special and relatable.

Perfection makes others want to see fault in you because they can't relate to it. It makes them feel shame and self-rejection. I know that's not what your heart wants others to feel, because those are exactly the same feelings you are trying to avoid. Open all the doors and windows to your life and let your essence out without any need to lessen its effect on the world.

Shine friends! The world needs to see your light. Let's all be human together.

Tip:
Rather than
see life as scary and
too big to come out and
show yourself, see it as an
exciting adventure that
you are going to
master!

To explore further, try these:

Stop:
- ✓ Masking your insecurities.
- ✓ Telling people you know more than you really do.
- ✓ Putting out emotions that don't reflect how you truly feel inside.
- ✓ Trying to convince people that you know it all and that they don't know anything.
- ✓ Defending yourself. Get to the truth by allowing the truth to be seen.
- ✓ Working on one area of your life and neglecting all of the other areas.
- ✓ Believing you will not be loved if you show the truth of who you are. That is a story we tell ourselves so that we don't have to change.
- ✓ Thinking you have control over what and how other people think of you.
- ✓ Trying to convince people to believe you. If what you say is authentic, it will naturally happen. You won't need to force it.
- ✓ Guarding your heart. You can feel what comes up. You are capable.
- ✓ Negative thinking. It will only make you want to hide more.
- ✓ Thinking you aren't enough and the world won't love the real you.
- ✓ Hiding information from people you love.

Start:
✓ Believing how you were created was meant to be.
✓ Getting excited to grow and trusting that it is natural to do so.
✓ Dreaming about where you would like to guide your life with the support of the Universe – CO-Create!
✓ Making conscious efforts to expose your insecurities.
✓ Allowing your emotions to be exposed and love the authenticity in it.
✓ Creating healthy relationships that will support the real you.
✓ Embracing your divine perfection. You were created to be you.
✓ Expressing with words how you really feel.
✓ Saying what you do know and allow what you don't know to be seen.
✓ Allowing people in that you can trust to see all the aspects of you.
✓ Cleaning out emotional closets. Allow the pain to release. Nothing needs to be hidden away.
✓ Saying what's hard to people so you aren't holding in the truth.
✓ Shine your gifts to the world so you don't have to carry the secret.

Make a list of the areas you struggle with the most.
1.
2.
3.
4.
5.

What steps will you take to improve those areas?
1.
2.
3.
4.
5.

How will your life be different when you implement these changes?

_____

_____

_____

_____

_____

Trapped Self

Bringing forward your authentic self can be a challenge, especially when you've worked so hard to hide it. But there are reasons for it. In therapy, I find some core causes of this desire to hide can be shame, guilt, oppression, unresolved issues, miscommunication, trust issues, or disrespect. You have to realize that the effects of these issues stay long after the obstacle has passed. It becomes a reflex.

Each and every time another threat shows up, you will find yourself automatically assuming it's the same threat as in past. To manage these threats, we retreat to a place of refuge to "stay safe." The problem is that unhealed wounds rarely feel safe, so we stay far too long.

When this occurs, we start to feel bad. We have feelings of boredom, annoyance, irritability, and an overall sense of "what's the point?" Lethargy and a sense of helplessness follow. Grief continues to well up and your ability to take action decreases the longer you stay in this place.

> *What keeps us trapped is the belief we have no choice.*

In psychology we call this "coping." It's doing what it takes to survive, but coping strategies are not meant to last forever. Eventually, the coping strategy will become less effective and more toxic than the original wound. You'll find yourself saying "I can't do it anymore!" That's the start of healing, so yippee! But sadly, it was forced upon you because you couldn't continue the struggle of holding it together anymore.

It's been said that most mental illness comes from staying strong too long. I want you to be able to choose. You should begin to see, when these feelings come up, that they are trying to tell you to start moving. The storm is over, so start sailing again! It's the only way to build a new life. Let the healing begin.

This can be so hard. I still struggle with this part, but each time it happens I become more graceful with the transition.

> *What you use to protect yourself can become your greatest enemy.*

Be conscious when these symptoms arise and be willing to take an honest inventory of your surroundings. Take the actions that you feel you can, and move forward. Sometimes the best you can do is grieve and let go. Other times you'll need to take an action step or say your truth. Or maybe you'll need to change an unhealthy behavior that must stop. Whatever it is, do it now because holding yourself back can't continue. You are precious and you were meant to shine!

Stop:
- ✓ Disassociating. If you catch yourself doing it, breathe and work on returning to your body.
- ✓ Listening to other people's opinions. Letting that be the reason you don't grow is a bad idea.
- ✓ Being something other than who you are. Authenticity is the key to freedom.
- ✓ Thinking you can change things outside of you to make the inside whole. To grow is an inside job.
- ✓ Looking for the destiny and remember the joy is being present in the journey.
- ✓ Thinking you are weak. You got this!
- ✓ Living in the past, hoping that it will fix your future. It won't work.
- ✓ Trying to stay safe, take a risk to free yourself.
- ✓ Holding onto the story. You think it, you create it.
- ✓ Thinking someone else is going to come and rescue you.
- ✓ Waiting. If you long for it, you will never have it.
- ✓ Reinforcing that the wound is the only truth. There are a lot of other realities.

✓ Trying to predict what will happen when you come out of your place of refuge.

✓ Setting conditions to come out. The Universe does not create conditions.

Start:

✓ Grounding yourself and working on truly staying present in the moment.

✓ Looking for the life that you want to create. As you do, allow it to gradually unfold.

✓ Choosing a path to take and follow it to the end. Don't stop when emotions get hard.

✓ Taking an honest inventory of your fears, looking at what is true fear and what is a false fear. Move forward accordingly.

✓ Knowing it's worth it to grow and leave your place of safety.

✓ Making the outcome bigger than you. Create a legacy that will touch lives.

✓ Looking for what is right and follow it to freedom.

✓ Getting as much love as you can from anywhere you know how. Love heals pain, like the sun raises the seeds from the earth.

✓ Trusting there is a meaning in life. There is a reason. Let it show itself to you over time by keeping a look out for it.

✓ Focusing on feeling stuck, that is a feeling not a fact.

✓ Looking at when the feelings of being trapped come up. It means you are staying too long.

✓ Believing that your suffering and pain can be over. Be as real as you can.

✓ Allowing the outside world to support you as you start to shine.

Make a list of the areas you struggle with the most.

1.

2.

3.

4.

5.

What steps will you take to improve those areas?

1.

2.

3.

4.

5.

How will your life be different when you implement these changes?

_____

_____

_____

_____

_____

Tip:
When you
are attracted to
something, it is likely
the aspect of yourself that
you have not allowed to
be free. Go inward
not out.

Energetic Walls

Energetic walls are shifty by nature, but their purpose is easy to understand. They control situations in our lives and shift our actions to protect the core essence. If you have pain trapped inside, for example, you are likely to find an energetic wall will pop up to when something threatens to cause you more pain. It's there to protect you. But left uncontrolled, energetic walls make a mess. In psychology we can call this denial or repression.

We know these energetic walls are there, but it isn't something you can literally see; we just see the effects of the wall. They will often create an under or over-compensation to life's challenges. So if Bob sees Susan, and she reminds him of a positive interaction with an old girlfriend, he will likely be attracted to her. But if Bob had a negative interaction with his ex-girlfriend, he will be likely try to avoid her. This has very little to do with Susan at all. Bob's reaction to Susan comes from an affected place in the past.

I want you to heal these life-shifting walls so that you can get back on course. Can see how these bumps in the road can be incredibly frustrating? Your unconscious mind is actually creating roadblocks to success. If you're someone who has to see the "why" of life, this becomes a very challenging hurdle to your evolution. More often than not, it takes someone from the outside to guide you inward to see where you are in your own way. I want you to *see* the evidence that there is a block inside of you. Watch for excesses and deficiencies in your life as verification of these internal walls.

Keep in mind that these walls can also show up in others. If you react to them, you reinforce them. Stay true to your course. Stay in integrity. Value the person and don't compromise your own value. The coolest part of all of this is that when you stay true to your path, you heal those who are off their path. Isn't that extraordinary? Honoring you also honors another. Once again, the gift of synthesis.

Tip: If life isn't giving you the outcome you are looking for, use this as a great reminder that denial or repression may be informing your outcome. Do some backtracking and investigation work. Keep an eye out for heartache! That's the target you are looking for.

Stop:
- ✓ Not trusting yourself. You have all the tools to go inward. You have to learn to use them.
- ✓ Focusing on fear. What you focus on, you create.
- ✓ Worrying about problems, it wastes necessary energy.
- ✓ Catastrophizing. You have to see what is, not what you want or are afraid of.
- ✓ Falling back into what is familiar.
- ✓ Listening to self-doubt.
- ✓ Thinking others know what is right for you. You are the only one who knows what is best for you.
- ✓ Thinking you have to see it for it to be true.
- ✓ Pushing forward when things don't work.
- ✓ Directing life to the goal you think it **should** be. Let it guide you to your dreams.
- ✓ Trying to stay ahead of the challenge. Be willing to experience it fully so it can heal.
- ✓ Allowing impulsive or compulsive behaviors to govern your life.
- ✓ Second-guessing every decision. Make a choice and ride it out until you have clarity.
- ✓ Believing there is only one way. There are infinite ways to the core of you.

Start:
- ✓ Talking kindly to yourself, encourage yourself to grow no matter what you face. The real you is needed in this world.
- ✓ Believing that it is possible, no matter the barriers.
- ✓ Putting one foot in front of another. Faithful steps create growth.
- ✓ Committing to your goals and follow through to the end. You are worth great outcomes.
- ✓ Trusting that it will be what it is meant to be.
- ✓ Tuning into your body and noticing what needs to change. Quietly adapt.
- ✓ Removing these walls one by one. Let nothing get in your way.
- ✓ Getting excited that there is more to you.

✓ Using your feelings as a guide to the neglected parts of who you are.

✓ Enjoying the treasure hunt of the hidden gold in you. See it as an adventure.

✓ Allowing your thoughts to be guided and redirected to a higher plane.

✓ Watching for thoughts that shift back and forth. This is the first sign you are getting close to one of the energetic walls.

✓ Learning to just be with it. Allow all resistance and clinging to dissipate, so the real you can emerge.

Make a list of the areas you struggle with the most.

1.

2.

3.

4.

5.

What steps will you take to improve those areas?

1.

2.

3.

4.

5.

How will your life be different when you implement these changes?

_____

_____

_____

_____

_____

Spiritualizing Your Emotions

Emotions, in general, are very challenging to navigate. Without spiritual principles, I've found they can feel all-consuming. Psychological distress and emotional flooding occurs when we are lacking the tools to handle the BIG job of navigating the ups and downs of our emotions.

And let's be clear: it's really quite tricky. For example, if you were raised in a loving environment, you may lack the skills to manage conflict. If you were raised in a critical environment you may be lacking the skills to navigate a loving relationship. Either experience leaves a gap to be filled by further life experiences.

If you refuse those circumstances as opportunities to grow, they become barriers to your success. The way you grow is by objectively looking at the situation without over-personalizing the occurrence. See it for what it is. Then look at your response or reaction to it. Did it create the outcome you desired, or did it create an outcome you didn't desire?

> *"Man learns through experience, and the spiritual path is full of different kinds of experiences. He will encounter many difficulties and obstacles, and they are the very experiences he needs to encourage and complete the cleansing process."*
> *- Sai Baba*

Try to see life as a school, where you go to grow and learn new perspectives. Think of the Universe as your instructor, using people, challenges, and experiences as the curriculum. Your life is meant to teach you lessons that will help you in the future and give you a chance to grow spiritually. If you're struggling with your emotions, try to see if your negative responses come from your inability to receive the teachings of the Universe.

The next step is to realize your potential. Imagine if you weren't hurting. How you would want to evolve based on these challenges? How would you move forward?

You can identify the correct path for you by observing and using discernment as your guide. The dictionary definition of discernment is "perception in the absence of judgment with a view to obtaining spiritual discretion and understanding." In practice, discernment is just another way to see what is not evident to the average mind. It is with discernment that you move forward, trusting that you are choosing what is best for your heart at that time.

One final note: always remember to come back to love after the lesson has been fully integrated into your life. Send out gratitude and release any emotional pain that is tied to the experience.

Tip: If you stay true to love, spiritual principles can become the magical gateway to freedom. Love eliminates fear!

You can work on this area by considering the following:

Stop:
- ✓ Thinking life has no rhyme or reason.
- ✓ Feeling threatened by life. Instead, embrace it as an adventure.
- ✓ Focusing on what could go wrong. Think of it as an opportunity to gain wisdom.
- ✓ Thinking you are RIGHT and focusing on how you have been wronged.
- ✓ Creating a story that leads you to a victim mindset or wounded place.
- ✓ Repeating patterns over and over.
- ✓ Staying in control, thinking you are the only master of your destiny.
- ✓ Believing that you can't handle something.
- ✓ Thinking that others are incapable. Everyone is capable.
- ✓ Trying to hold things together.
- ✓ Trying to do it all on your own. We all need support.
- ✓ Being closed minded. Others perspectives may just be the key to your freedom.

✓ Thinking someone else's success can be an exact template to your success. The reason for their success was that they were true to their heart.

✓ Thinking you can spiritually bypass emotions.

✓ Taking things personally. It's not happening to hurt you.

Start:

✓ Looking for "higher ground." Consider principles that could lead you to a greater capacity to love and to be loved.

✓ Making a choice to change and committing to it.

✓ Opening your mind to infinite possibilities.

✓ Letting things fall apart so they can find the correct order, not your order.

✓ Looking for great spiritual teachers. Those who are here now or those whose work has been documented.

✓ Integrating rather than eliminating.

✓ Writing out your reactions to your challenges. Look at them and explore if they are working for you.

✓ Witnessing success in others. Take those lessons and integrate their wisdom into your personalized blessings.

✓ Creating a garden of knowledge and sharing it with the world by bearing fruit.

✓ Experiencing rather than resisting.

✓ Seeing challenges like a rainstorm—once they are over, a rainbow appears and a fresh start begins.

✓ Understanding the concept that nothing is permanent.

✓ Allowing the true understanding of "This too shall pass."

Make a list of the areas you struggle with the most.

1.

2.

3.

4.

5.

What steps will you take to improve those areas?

1.

2.

3.

4.

5.

How will your life be different when you implement these changes?

_____

_____

_____

_____

_____

Tip: Try doing something the way a friend would do it, rather than the way you would normally do it. Then watch to see what happens.

Take an honest assessment of where you stand in these areas

Scoring guide:

1 = I realize there's a problem

2 = I have contemplated the issue

3 = I have considered actions steps for the issue

4 = I am prepared to take action

5 = I am taking necessary action steps

6 = I am taking action and I have already made some mistakes

7 = I am integrating lessons from failed action steps

8 = I am making adaptations to my actions

9 = I am being consistent in the actions needed

10 = I am at my ideal goal, I just need to maintain it

The Emotional Body

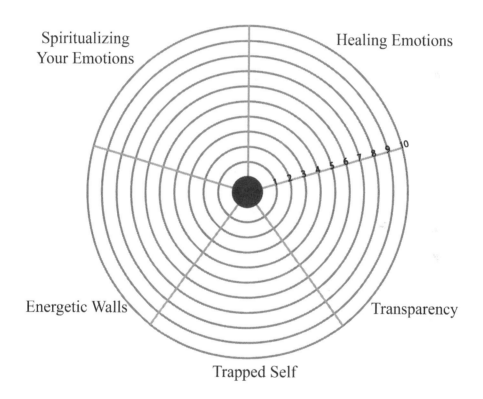

CHAPTER SEVEN

The Physical Body

Your physical body is the bridge between the higher planes and earth. You need to become attuned to your body so the higher and lower aspects of your self can flow and relay messages back and forth effortlessly. Even though it's quite tangible, there is still a lot to learn and discover about how the physical body affects our entire "self."

We still need to connect to our physical body in order to grow. Consider exercising, eating, attuning, balancing, and realigning as ways you can connect with your physical body. As you regain control over your body, you regain a connection to all that is. Remember the mind, body,

> *"A healthy body is a guest-chamber for the soul; a sick body is a prison."*
>
> *Francis Bacon*

spirit connection is essential for optimal health. If any one of those is disregarded, then it's like breaking a circuit. The messages will not relay clearly and you will find yourself out of alignment.

Force of Habit

This is no easy task and a lazy mind is the greatest saboteur of all. But you have the strength to overcome your bad habits if you are ready to fall in love with you. Most of us have created tricks to tell ourselves that working in these areas is not love. Just because it's hard doesn't mean it's not love. The fact is, we can get addicted to hurting ourselves very easily.

Break out of that habit and you may find you really are someone worth loving.

In my earlier years, I had a core fear of public speaking and having attention focused on me. It was really just one of those bad habits I had developed and could overcome. I remember sitting at Western Oregon University and loving my courses. I particularly remember loving the people, my classmates, just for who they were. I loved this safe and open learning environment.

When it came time to give presentations, that all changed. I would often inform my professors that I was unwilling to do so and would even drop the course or take a big fat "F" rather than expose my cowardly self. This always baffled my classmates. They knew me as jovial and friendly, attracting attention in my own way. Why was I unwilling to do so in front of the room?

My friends would ask me, "Why won't you speak in front of people? You would be the best of the best!" They were surprised to learn that I had a fear of public speaking. The truth of the matter was that none of them really knew that I had trauma underneath and that the core of this trauma was that somebody hurt me when I was exposed. Hiding seemed like the practical solution – in fact, a BRILLIANT solution to prevent the wounded little girl from being exposed.

Near the end of my time there, I was in a research class. It was time to announce the subject of our final project and I was out of ideas. My friend and I were sitting in the back of the room waiting for our turn to explain our project. We had nothing.

When our professor called on us, much to my surprise, an idea just popped out of me. I said, "I think we should do a project on lavender essential oil and how it changes people's mood." My professor beamed and said "Oh, my God! That's brilliant." Later she took me aside, telling me that we needed more research behind this idea and that we should definitely do a study.

As the project progressed, I found that I really did enjoy the research, though it was not my area of strength. I also agreed to do the project with the one stipulation to my research partner: that I would not have to speak publicly. The professor agreed to take us on and said that she thought we could publish our work. That was exciting to me, so I agreed.

This was turning out to be the best of both worlds. I had the opportunity to actually publish scientific research, and I was thrilled to have no pressure to perform publicly. Then two weeks before presentation time, my professor turned to me and announced, "Lisa, you have to speak or I will not publish this." As you can imagine, my heart dropped, my face flushed, and terror erupted in my body.

For the next two weeks, I was petrified and absolutely refused to make a public presentation. My project partner reminded me that I <u>had</u> to do this, since she needed the credit as well. Being the people pleaser that I was, I felt trapped in a dichotomy that offered no escape.

From this point on, sleep was out the door and diarrhea was arriving frequently. I dreaded the looming horror of being exposed. All I would commit to was reading a portion of the report to the attending students, a population of about 100 people. I would go through the fire for my people!

Presentation day arrived and I stood in front of the crowd with every part of my body shaking. When it was my time to speak, even though I felt like I was going to throw up, it was only words that started to come out my mouth. Surprisingly, I sounded pretty good. In fact, it flowed fairly well.

I completed my part and sat down. I was supposed to run the PowerPoint for my friend's portion of the presentation, but that's when my brain went out the door and I completely screwed up her section, almost bringing her to tears. Thank God my friend forgave me!

And thank God Dr. Strapp forced me to perform. She was the first person who challenged my bad habit of non-performance and proved to me that I could survive. Guess what? I now spend a great deal of my professional life in the role of "public speaker." No one is more surprised than I.

Physical Exercise

Physical exercise is a significant part of awakening the health of your body as well as releasing built-up toxins. When you exercise you are creating inertia (effort, motion, and action) and when one thing starts to move, everything starts to move.

Grief, joy, sickness, creativity, and pain are all stored in the warehouse of "you." If you get moving, you will see that action shift you forward and support you in the next stage of your life. Creativity will begin to spark and you may be surprised when you discover your unseen potential. A stagnant lifestyle will elicit feelings of lethargy and self-doubt. We are meant to grow as living beings. If you are not growing forward, then you will not create your desired outcome.

The research is clear that exercise outperforms antidepressants by a long shot. The greatest gift of exercise is that it allows you to pass challenging emotions through the body rather than filtering them through the mind or adding too much stress on the heart. Exercise is the natural way to literally move you through challenging times.

Take one step at a time. If you've become stagnant, changing patterns and developing consistency takes time. It may be uncomfortable at first. Most important things are. If you've become addicted to harmful behaviors, you can only change those behaviors by taking responsibility for the parts of yourself that are running amuck.

> *"An early-morning walk is a blessing for the whole day."*
>
> *Henry David Thoreau*

I discovered the power of exercise through the process of being pissed at my partner. We were having a difficult time and I had an inner demon that needed to be released. We had some backed up resentment that needed to be worked through, but I wasn't taking any personal responsibility for it. I knew in my heart of hearts that I was in love with my partner, but every time I found myself next to her I would spew venomous verbal vomit on her.

I understood that this was a bad choice, but it took a while for me to realize that going for a walk might be a good strategic plan to get back to the path of love. As I did, my chest started to expand. I felt stronger and the emotions that were making me feel weak were released. I thought to myself "What a great idea. I don't have to do emotions through rage or tears or internal battles. I can just walk it off!" That was also much easier on us both.

This was the beginning of me taking small, incremental steps in exercising as a way to process emotions and keep the gift of movement and circulation flowing through my life. Now, any time I feel stagnation, I remember that lesson and I try to give myself motion again. It was the simple steps, the decision to leave the house, the decision to move, and the decision to go back towards love, that showed me that every forward step I take brings me to more love.

Tip: Just start and make it a habit; one step at a time. It will get easier!

So consider these ways to make shifts in this area:

Stop:
- ✓ Saying I will start tomorrow. You have to use the moment to kick start change.
- ✓ Creating reasons you can't. There will always be a reason why not. Look for how you can instead.
- ✓ Thinking it is hard. It may well be, but think instead of ways to empower yourself to take the first step.
- ✓ Focusing on why you don't want to do it.
- ✓ Prioritizing other things over your health.
- ✓ Dreading it. Remember it is a gift.
- ✓ Thinking you need energy to begin. Exercise will create it.
- ✓ Thinking it is too expensive.
- ✓ Allowing an injury or disability to stop you. Find new ways to be physical.
- ✓ Thinking you have to be comfortable to exercise.

✓ Thinking you need to have a partner to motivate you.

✓ Thinking you have to know what to do. Ask others who are successful at it.

Start:

✓ Getting excited for change!

✓ Taking it one day at a time.

✓ Getting creative on ways to exercise.

✓ Finding others who are exercising.

✓ Finding a place that feels easy to exercise. Identify a place where you can be real – where you don't need to put up a false image.

✓ Coming up with ideas that you can do at home.

✓ Creating measurable goals.

✓ Committing to consistency.

✓ Taking small steps each day.

✓ Making it fun and looking for creative ways to make it enjoyable.

✓ Joining a team of people doing similar self-care.

✓ Getting the right clothes and shoes to make it comfortable.

✓ Finding the music that will inspire and motivate you.

Make a list of the areas you struggle with the most.

1.

2.

3.

4.

5.

What steps will you take to improve those areas?

1.

2.

3.

4.

5.

How will your life be different when you implement these changes?

_____

_____

_____

_____

_____

Eating and Drinking Right

Food is energy; it's that simple. We ingest it and our body uses it to live, repair, and grow. By balancing your food intake, you will in return balance your overall physical health. But what does dietary balance look like?

Allow yourself the foods you want in moderation. Listen to what you are craving. Ask yourself, "Is this a healthy craving or an avoidance craving?" Stop focusing on the idea of what is bad and what is good or you will place a negative charge upon your food. Remember the key here is balance, not restriction or indulgence. Remember too, that water is crucial to keeping our lives in flow. If something is stagnant, water is what starts it moving.

If you live in the U.S., you know we are a nation addicted to regulating food intake. This in itself causes much greater issues than having a "treat" now and then. Your body is reading behavior patterns to know how to stay in homeostasis. On/off behaviors create havoc in our overall health and our balance.

> *Your food is your fuel for life; does it reflect health or sickness?*

I remember standing in the shower one day and looking down and realizing my six-pack was in the fridge. What replaced it was blocking the view of my feet. It was at this point that I realized I needed to do a self-evaluation of what was going into my body.

A few days later, I read an article that said that if you are drinking three sodas a day, over a one-year period that choice adds something like 72-pounds of weight to your body. I thought, "Oh dear God! Houston we have a problem!" I made a decision to start looking at what could be the chief saboteur of my overall health and well-being. It was me.

I cut out soda and moved to iced tea, I stopped drinking creamer in my coffee and just started to pay more attention to my overall intake of food and drink. It was amazing. Soon my toes started to appear. I started to feel more energy in my body and I felt my essence start to be honored again. I felt a little more love. I didn't realize that what I had been doing was filling myself with emptiness. Sometimes just becoming conscious of the things you are doing is the doorway back to love.

Tip:
Make a food log for a week and take a deeper look at your desires for food. See if what you are doing is regulating your desires or managing them. Regulating is to control and managing is to take charge of, or care for. It's a fine line that you really need to pay attention to.

So consider this as you start to move forward:

Stop:
- ✓ Judging how you eat. Negative thoughts affect how your body processes food.
- ✓ Withholding what you want from yourself. Withholding creates a disconnection from your true feelings. It has also been found to raise the desire for what is being withheld.
- ✓ Avoiding food. It's your fuel.
- ✓ Allowing other people's beliefs to override what is best for you.
- ✓ Telling yourself you're not perfect as you are. Trying to be someone other than you are will create suffering.
- ✓ Creating the ideas that you need more than what is comfortable. Eat to the point that feels right and no more. Be conscious of what you put in your body.

✓ Overriding your knowing of when you have had enough.
✓ Depriving yourself by dieting or withholding food from yourself.
✓ Hiding what you eat.
✓ Stuffing your emotions with food.
✓ Creating specialness through food.

Start:
✓ Listening to your body and what it wants.
✓ Noticing what positively and negatively affects your body and make adjustments accordingly.
✓ Seeking foods you enjoy and that you know are healthy. Build a lifestyle that honors good choices.
✓ Looking for healthy substitutes for harmful foods.
✓ Looking up new recipes for a balanced lifestyle.
✓ Investing in healthy classes and teachings that support growth in your eating habits.
✓ Allowing rewards each week as you succeed and know that treats can be a <u>part</u> of your overall food plan, rather than the whole.
✓ Sharing your healthy habits with friends.
✓ Positive self-talk and know that you are investing in your life in a loving and positive way.
✓ Thinking ahead for food prep so that you don't make impulsive choices.
✓ Asking those who have succeeded what worked for them, and learn from the pieces that might help you.

Make a list of the areas you struggle with the most.
1.
2.
3.
4.
5.

What steps will you take to improve them?

1.

2.

3.

4.

5.

How will your life be different when you implement these changes?

_____

_____

_____

_____

_____

<u>Sleeping Well</u>

Sleeping well is imperative to your overall health. Long-term lack of sleep can cause real mental illness and even lead to death in extreme cases. You must set yourself up for success by getting the proper amount of sleep. Anything that stops you from getting a healthy night's sleep must go.

Begin by addressing any issues with sleep disturbances with your doctor or mental health therapist. Then, examine your dreams and work toward interpreting their underlying meanings. Ultimately, you must find the amount of sleep that is right for you to feel energized. Once you discover that right amount, settle for nothing less.

> *"Think in the morning. Act in the noon. Eat in the evening. Sleep in the night."*
> *William Blake*

One major cause of sleep disturbances is the fear of letting go. When you fall asleep you have to let go of control. But at times we hang onto thoughts as a method of control. We control our thoughts so our pain doesn't bubble up to the surface. If you are struggling with racing thoughts, it's an indicator that you may have some grief or challenging emotions that you are avoiding. Doing your healing work is imperative and you need to put this at the top of your priority list if sleep is being disrupted.

Warning: Medications can be masking the real issue. Do not stop them without a professional to work with you on this topic, but actively work on the root of the issue so that eventually you can wean off of them. I want you to heal fully, not to delay and avoid the symptoms. Remember to listen to your body and to work with it until you get to the core of the issue. Don't think ignoring the warning lights on your ship is a good idea; it's not!

Tip: Create a pattern of behavior that you do on a regular basis that will tell your brain it's time to start closing down shop. Take a bath, stop eating a couple of hours before bed time, and turn the TV off!

Here are some ideas to consider as you seek to improve your sleep health:

Stop:
- ✓ Staying up too late. Don't allow your partner or yourself to keep you up too long.
- ✓ Saying there is too much to do.
- ✓ Avoiding going to the doctor.
- ✓ Ignoring your dreams.
- ✓ Rushing around until it's time to go to bed.
- ✓ Settling for not enough sleep.
- ✓ Getting addicted to medications that cause a false state of rest.
- ✓ Oversleeping.
- ✓ Avoiding things by sleeping.

- ✓ Taking naps that are too long.
- ✓ Drinking too much caffeine.
- ✓ Eating or drinking late at night.
- ✓ Exercising too late at night.
- ✓ Racing thoughts. Ground yourself and meditate to calm your mind, if needed.
- ✓ Trying to put everything into a box in your head.

Start:
- ✓ Going to bed on time.
- ✓ Listening to your body for how much sleep you need.
- ✓ Practicing the same pre-sleep rituals that encourage restful sleep.
- ✓ Allowing for naps if needed (short and sweet).
- ✓ Creating an honoring, comfortable space for sleep.
- ✓ Allowing outside support when you run out of options to sleep.
- ✓ Considering natural supplements rather than synthetic ones.
- ✓ Keeping a dream journal.
- ✓ Allowing yourself more downtime before bed to unwind.
- ✓ Seeing sleep as just as important as awake time.
- ✓ Going to bed and waking up at the same time.
- ✓ Focusing on your breathing and stretching before bed.

Make a list of the areas you struggle with the most.
1.
2.
3.
4.
5.

What steps will you take to improve those areas?
1.
2.
3.
4.
5.

How will your life be different when you implement these changes?

_____

_____

_____

_____

_____

Honoring Your Physical Appearance

There are times in life we basically let ourselves go. We listen to the nagging internal dialog that reminds us of how we fall short of others and spend our time wishing we were different than what we really are. Find what makes you feel true to you.

If you want comfortable, find comfortable, but do it with your full effort. If you want to feel sexy or confident (or any other state) bring the inside to the outside or the outside to the inside. Give yourself all the attention you deserve and you will find that it is the answer to feeling more true to you.

Are you a rock star on the inside? Create it on the outside. Are you ready to be a confident business person? Step into the clothes that bring that state and feeling out in you.

However you prefer to do it, bring more of *you* into this world. Express it out loud! If you are unwilling to do this personal expression work, your light will be dimmed. If all you are doing is feeling disgust for yourself, you won't have the energy for anything productive. Be your best and you will feel your best. Now that's productive!

To stand in your beauty takes great confidence. To sit in your insecurities leads to a feeling of defeat.

It took time for me to get the hang of this. I had to do what made me feel good and not do what made others thought made me look good. It had to be 100% for me. In the end it has been really empowering and it will be for you as well. You will love what you become.

Think of the feeling you get when you see a certain person that is delicious and irresistible to you. Can you imagine how extraordinary it would be if that's how you felt when you looked at yourself in the mirror?

Tip: Every day, look in the mirror and instead of saying something that isn't loving, say something like "I see the beauty in you and I welcome more of you to return to me."

To explore this area of growth, consider the following:

Stop:
✓ Trying to "measure up."
✓ Denying your value.
✓ Acting incapable of honoring your physical appearance.
✓ Dressing down because you are afraid of the attention you may receive.
✓ Dressing like you are someone that you are not.
✓ Letting someone else pick your look.
✓ Skimping on the amount of time and money you put into yourself.
✓ Thinking negatively about yourself.
✓ Thinking you can't improve.
✓ Believing your looks have anything to do with someone else's opinion.
✓ Saying there isn't enough time.
✓ Saying you are too tired to put in the effort.

Start:
✓ Giving yourself an extra 10 minutes each day to get ready.
✓ Finding clothes that make you feel more confident.
✓ Investing money and time in your outer appearance.
✓ Telling yourself you are a beautiful being and perfect just the way you are.
✓ Looking for things that make you zing.
✓ Getting excited to create your personal artistic flare through the expression of your outer canvas.
✓ Finding physical expressions that awaken your inner feelings.
✓ Trusting you are meant to shine to the outer world.
✓ Aligning with what you know is in your heart.
✓ Forgetting the "shoulds" and "have tos" and be who you really are.

Make a list of the areas you struggle with the most.
1.
2.
3.
4.
5.

What steps will you take to improve those areas?
1.
2.
3.
4.
5.

How will your life be different when you implement these changes?

_____

_____

_____

_____

_____

Honoring Your Time

Time-related issues are probably the number one complaint I hear in my office. There either isn't enough time or we are bored because there is too much of it. Few mention the amount of "now" they have. We have to discover our true relationship to time.

I remember asking a shaman friend of mine what I could do when I felt pressured by time. He suggested I could bring magic into time by coming into the moment. I realized he was telling me that time has no limits in the moment.

In hypnotherapy, we stretch time out for long periods even though it may be literally just a few minutes. Think of how much time we throw away by daydreaming of the past or the future and never being in the present moment. You can bring magic into your life by training your mind, body, and spirit to stay present no matter what.

Ultimately, time is linked to choice. How do you manage your choices and what are you prioritizing? It still makes me curious to see how far off our path we can move and rationalize it by saying we just don't have time to make the appropriate adjustments.

It's not uncommon for clients to plop on my couch and say, "There's just not enough time!" I always pause my clients right in the middle of their speech and I say, "Hold that feeling in your body for just a minute." And the inevitable reply is, "What feeling?" I hold my hand over their heart and they start to cry and realize that they have skipped over all the parts of their lives that are hurting. They've deleted parts of themselves.

> *To fall under the illusion of time by believing there is not enough or too much is how we hypnotize ourselves out of being in the moment.*

When we complain about time issues, we're really just using time as an excuse. The truth of the matter is we don't want to take time to love ourselves. We don't want to take time to think about what really matters. We don't want to look at what's hurting us. We want to pretend that we're not hurt.

You may be someone who doesn't take time for yourself, or you may be someone that doesn't take time for others. True balance means

109

remembering that loving the self AND others is how we keep our buoyancy. One without the other sinks our ship. Then you get to do years of work with your therapist to figure out how to bring it back to the surface. Skip the sinking!

Tip: Master staying in the moment! Use a bell or an alarm to remind you to come back and center. The moment is where the gold is!

Here are a few things you need to consider as you seek a healthy perspective on time:

Stop:
- ✓ Making excuses for why there isn't enough time.
- ✓ Avoiding the present moment. Be in it.
- ✓ Creating false ideas of time. Saying "I'll get to it in the future," is not getting to it.
- ✓ Wasting time. (e.g., screen time, sleeping, worrying)
- ✓ Acting like you have all the time in the world.
- ✓ Not prioritizing or using your time unwisely.
- ✓ Working on other people's time schedules.
- ✓ Using time as an excuse.
- ✓ Day dreaming.
- ✓ Focusing on what could happen.
- ✓ Thinking you aren't worth taking time for.

Start:
- ✓ Training your mind to stay in the present moment.
- ✓ Exploring ways you can create magic in the moment.

✓ Trusting that you are the driver of your life and that you can stay in charge of your destiny.

✓ Using time as an opportunity to empower yourself. Let it support you.

✓ Remembering that time is an investment in you.

✓ Using schedules as a way to stay true to your intentions. Make sure you hold space for what you want to accomplish.

✓ Prioritizing your needs and building them into manageable chunks.

✓ Believing you are worth more time.

✓ Getting creative in manifesting space in your life.

✓ Trusting others and believing they are capable. Then you can focus on your priorities.

✓ Moving beyond what you know and exploring other ways of managing time.

Make a list of the areas you struggle with the most.
1.
2.
3.
4.
5.

What steps will you take to improve those areas?
1.
2.
3.
4.
5.

How will your life be different when you implement these changes?

_____

_____

_____

_____

_____

Take an honest assessment of where you stand in these areas

Scoring guide:

1 = I realize there's a problem

2 = I have contemplated the issue

3 = I have considered actions steps for the issue

4 = I am prepared to take action

5 = I am taking necessary action steps

6 = I am taking action and I have already made some mistakes

7 = I am integrating lessons from failed action steps

8 = I am making adaptations to my actions

9 = I am being consistent in the actions needed

10 = I am at my ideal goal, I just need to maintain it

Physical Body

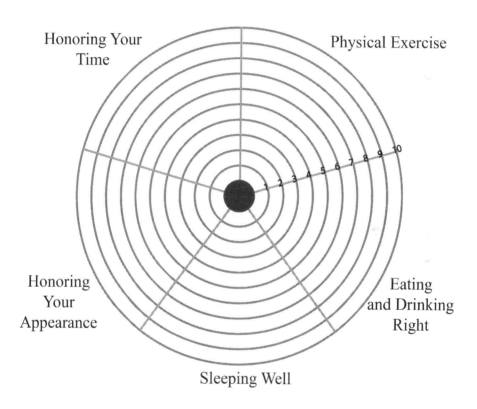

CHAPTER EIGHT

Mastering Love

The words "In Love" are important in this chapter. But we need to understand that phrase better. To be "In Love" is to be invested in manifesting more love in this world or coming from a place of love. We must become love. Nothing will grow without love.

Loving Yourself and Others

It should not surprise you that to live a balanced life you have to love yourself as much as you love others and vice-versa. Some want to give the world every ounce of what they have because they want to be worthy. Others want to take everything others have because they are afraid they won't have enough by themselves.

Embrace the idea that we are all "good enough." There is nothing to prove or to earn. We don't need to take from others. We are all equal and equally valuable.

I often teach that the Universe wants to fill our hearts and souls with abundance but we don't meet the Universe at the place that would allow that to happen. The Universe is reaching down to the earthly plane to touch you. Use love to lift your heart and soul up to the Universe.

> *"There is no charm equal to tenderness of heart."*
> Jane Austen

Unconditional love creates a life that values all human beings. You are a human being just like the rest of us! You need to align with the greater plan or you will be holding yourself back from your full potential.

The ultimate goal is to love what is. If you can't love another, it's because they are mirroring an aspect of yourself that you haven't integrated into your life. Take time to look at your judgments of others and yourself. Know that your ability to see the greater purpose in all things will free your spirit to create your best life now.

> Tip:
> When you find
> the perfect balance of
> loving what is and seeing the
> value of self and others equally,
> you will embody a state of
> being that will reflect
> contentment and
> peace.

Consider the following for growth in this area:

Stop:
- ✓ Positioning yourself as better than or less than others.
- ✓ Acting as if you have no value.
- ✓ Treating others better than yourself.
- ✓ Creating reasons you <u>must</u> give, even when it hurts you.
- ✓ Trying to earn your worth. You are already worthy.
- ✓ Trying to make your worth. It doesn't come from things or doing.
- ✓ Hiding your true identity.
- ✓ Trying to get someone to give to you, when they don't want to.
- ✓ Putting anyone in front of yourself.
- ✓ Hoping others will fill you.
- ✓ Creating reasons why you have to keep trying to make something work that clearly doesn't.
- ✓ Doing more than your part.
- ✓ Trying to make the world look the way you want. See the world the way it is.

Start:

✓ Loving yourself as you are.

✓ Embodying yourself rather than withholding from yourself.

✓ Trusting that you are meant for great things in your life.

✓ Trusting that everyone is worthy of greatness, including you.

✓ Exploring your needs and wants.

✓ Allowing people into your life who want to support your needs and wants.

✓ Anticipating greatness.

✓ Making space for a new life.

✓ Creating an inventory of places you have undervalued yourself and others and make change.

✓ Changing your wants and longings into excitement and anticipation.

Make a list of the areas you struggle with the most.

1.

2.

3.

4.

5.

What steps will you take to improve those areas?

1.

2.

3.

4.

5.

How will your life be different when you implement these changes?

_____

_____

_____

_____

_____

Loving Your Family and/or Partner

Our closest relationships are the most profound mirrors of our lives. Sometimes they reflect a painful experience; other times they reflect the beauty that we struggle to see within ourselves. Finding the perfect balance within these relationships is vital to our evolutionary process. The way we do this is by understanding that we need to experience these relationships **in** love.

Some of us have healthier relationships with our families and partners than others. It's important to navigate our lives in a way that holds love around those relationships so that we, in turn, fall in love with our self. Learning to love what **is,** without the need to shift or change people is what will give you ultimate peace within. By doing so, you will love all reflections of yourself.

Sometimes we need to step back from others when fear or anger floods our system. This will allow you to move inward and explore the wound in you that they have triggered. Each day that you learn to unconditionally love those around you, you free yourself from the chains of self-hate. In doing so, we bring a greater love to our world.

> *To love and allow another to be as they are creates a mirror image that reflects unconditional love back to the self.*

In Chapter Seven, I described a time in my relationship where I wasn't being very loving to my partner. I wanted the problem to be about her, but it was about me. I've learned that this kind of projection is both a subconscious and unconscious curse. We destroy what we love by avoiding loving ourselves.

That's why I committed to love instead of trying to be the best partner or the best person or trying to be good enough to deserve love. Love is my mission, and when I love others AND myself, I find peace.

Because we know that the outer world is a mirror of our internal world, we can see our self-love by how we treat others. When we're not loving another human being, we're really not loving ourselves.

Be willing to step back and allow your partner or your colleagues or your children to have space. In doing so, we allow space for our pain and we release the feelings of being trapped. Release the need to analyze. Release the need to be wounded. We all deserve great big love! Give yourself the space to let it in.

Tip: See someone in your family that you struggle with. Look through a lens of love at them and then say to yourself, your own name and say I love you as you are. i.e.,"Lisa, I love you as you are." You may be surprised by just how fast they are easier to connect to.

Consider these areas for growth:

Stop:
- ✓ Thinking people are just mean.
- ✓ Trying to figure out why they are doing what they are doing.
- ✓ Focusing on the problem.
- ✓ Believing you have to work everyone's problems out with them. You just need to love them and move forward.
- ✓ Trying to change people.
- ✓ Trying to stop others from making you feel the way they do. Take responsibility for your own feelings.
- ✓ Delaying change.
- ✓ Acting like you are incapable of handling people or your environment.
- ✓ Trying to convince people that they should be different than they are.
- ✓ Emotional cutoffs. Just move forward with love.
- ✓ Thinking that you are right and others are wrong.
- ✓ Thinking you have to fix someone. They are not broken.
- ✓ Withholding love.

Start:

✓ Trusting the flow of life.

✓ Believing everyone is whole and complete.

✓ Believing that everyone is capable.

✓ Looking at your own choices.

✓ Creating the destiny you want.

✓ Adjusting boundaries to help you stay in love.

✓ Taking 100% responsibility for your happiness.

✓ Seeing the lessons that come to you as a blessing.

✓ Allowing your feelings to come up when you are triggered.

✓ Holding unconditional love around yourself and others.

✓ Showing your love at all times.

Make a list of the areas you struggle with the most.

1.

2.

3.

4.

5.

What steps will you take to improve those areas?

1.

2.

3.

4.

5.

How will your life be different when you implement these changes?

_____

_____

_____

_____

_____

Loving Your Community

Your community is here to help you develop, and assist and support you in your growth process. Throughout the years I have seen many communities rise and fall. We need to understand that this is all part of the greater plan.

Your community is here to offer you something now. Find it. And when it's gone, you need to allow it to go, knowing another one is on the horizon. Don't cling to it or think that the community is the answer. It is the support or mold to hold you in place until you are ready to expand beyond that mold.

Love your community as it is and trust that every time you begin the birthing process of a new aspect of you, you will again move beyond the structures on which you once depended. In other words, as you grow, you will mature into new communities.

> *Community is the opportunity to explore deeper levels of myself.*

Each time a new community comes into your life, think about how extraordinary is it to have others to share in your growth experience. If you are avoiding letting others see your journey, then it may be that you are afraid to look like a novice. This will only get you so far.

Eventually you will find that the Universe will force you into change, whether you like it or not, and it often uses community interaction to do it. This is called fate. It's actually quite freeing not needing to have all the answers. Let communities help you and teach you. You will see.

Tip:
Look online for community groups or throw it out on Facebook that you are looking for a specific kind of group. There are a lot to choose from and I know you will find just what you need if you look.

You can grow your love for your community by exploring these ideas:

Stop:
- ✓ Holding onto structures that don't serve you.
- ✓ Isolating and thinking you don't need anyone.
- ✓ Thinking you need to prove your gift to anyone. Allow it to be seen because you are expressing your gift, not because you are trying to convince someone it is there.
- ✓ Fearing judgment.
- ✓ Holding on or clinging.
- ✓ Believing you are not valuable.
- ✓ Seeking approval.
- ✓ Living in roles and hierarchy.
- ✓ Acting like you have all the answers.
- ✓ Being territorial and becoming competitive or cliquish.
- ✓ Creating alliances to feel strong. When you work against someone you actually feel weak.

Start:
- ✓ Reaching out to like minds.
- ✓ Allowing the true you out.
- ✓ Creating opportunities to bring people together.
- ✓ Trusting that the Universe has a greater plan and that you may need more love around you.
- ✓ Trusting that you are more.
- ✓ Allowing people to cheer you on.
- ✓ Being authentic with your peers.
- ✓ Creating opportunity for community.
- ✓ Loving others as they are.
- ✓ Seeing the value in love and support.
- ✓ Allowing your community to be human. Make room for mistakes.
- ✓ Making space for multiple perspectives.

Make a list of the areas you struggle with the most.
1.
2.
3.
4.
5.

What steps will you take to improve those areas?
1.
2.
3.
4.
5.

How will your life be different when you implement these changes?

_____

_____

_____

_____

_____

Loving Your Universe – Your Higher Power

This is the foundation of all the steps we have talked about through this book. We know our brain is only using a fraction of its full potential. In the same way, the universe we can see is just a fraction of its full existence. Believe that there is far more to you than you know. Believe there is more to the Universe than you to know.

Just like a baby who comes into this world with a lifetime of growth ahead, you too have a lifetime of growing ahead of you. The faith we all innately have that we will grow until we die is the same faith we need to have in this knowing of something greater than us. Some

> *"Where the spirit does not work with the hand there is no art."*
>
> *Leonardo da Vinci*

things are bigger than we can see or understand and we must have faith that something has a greater interest in us than even we do.

Call it God, or Truth, or the Cosmic Force—it is there. Needing to understand it or create structure around it can limit its potential to work through us. Just believe and you will see.

I was raised in a conservative Christian home but I have found peace in embracing all religions, spiritual principles, and even science and pure potential as my higher power. I utilize all these modalities to connect to my higher source in infinite ways.

Whatever and however you do it for yourself is the right way for you. Just make a practice of connecting with it and you'll see great rewards from plugging into your own fueling station.

> Tip:
> Start working with the energy that you connect with. This may be by creating a sacred space or a place that is already created where you can be in relationship with this energy. Church, nature, even a quiet place in your home can be a great start.

You can explore this area by considering the following:

Stop:
- ✓ Doubting yourself. Believe that you are the director of your life.
- ✓ Limiting your potential.
- ✓ Putting bars of beliefs around this higher essence.
- ✓ Thinking you don't have to have a relationship with the Universe.
- ✓ Believing that you don't need the Universe. "I got this" is a poor foundation for growth.
- ✓ Thinking you are alone and not connected to something greater.
- ✓ Thinking that the Universe doesn't want to create with you.

✓ Thinking that it doesn't want to have a relationship with you.
✓ Thinking that you know better than someone else. It's a personal relationship, unique to each individual.
✓ Treating it like it isn't sacred.
✓ Acting like you aren't hungry for more.
✓ Thinking you can find it outside of you.
✓ Thinking you can outwit it.
✓ Fighting its love.
✓ Thinking it wants to punish you.
✓ Thinking it supports you when you are hurting yourself or others.

Start:
✓ Expecting more love to come in.
✓ Letting go. You are supported.
✓ Knowing that life is easier than you are making it.
✓ Being in awe of its potential.
✓ Letting life reflect your expansiveness back to you.
✓ Trusting that the Universe sees things you can't see and that it knows the greater plan.
✓ Having faith life will work itself out when you let it guide you.
✓ Coming back to the heart where this higher essence lives.
✓ Letting the Universe do its part.
✓ Having faith in something other than yourself.
✓ Looking for where you can find it in your world.

Make a list of the areas you struggle with the most.
1.
2.
3.
4.
5.

What steps will you take to improve those areas?
1.
2.

3.

4.

5.

How will your life be different when you implement these changes?

_____

_____

_____

_____

_____

<u>Loving What Is</u>

By loving what is, you are able to embrace life as it was meant to be. You no longer need to resist or cling to the things over which you have no control. You are here, now. That means you are able to enjoy life rather than feel like a victim of life. You can let go of pain and come back to your natural self. You can allow others to be as they are, because you would know what a blessing it is to just be. You can trust the unfolding of life, since you know it is the path you were meant to walk.

The reason that so many of us do not allow this to happen is we have been trained to not know who we are. In fact, we are terrified of who we really are. We have separated from our core selves in such a way that we have become strangers to our true identities.

To face the separated-self evokes great resistance—that is until we see this great riddle of life as a puzzle. The pieces are each of immense value. They create our wholeness. The veil that we build to stop ourselves from seeing who we really are is dropped when we summon the courage that comes from loving what is.

Boldly face life without controlling it. Let it happen. Let go of the pain that life evokes and keep moving forward. That doesn't mean you let someone hurt you or continue to do so forever more. No, it means you stay true to your heart. It becomes your guide. You trust it. When it hurts, you keep your heart open and you move forward. You stay true to you and love what is. As you do, you become empowered to love yourself as a part of life that is far more complex than our minds can understand.

Once you move all your illusion out of the way, you start to collaborate with the Universe. And when you are totally in the moment, you can hear the guidance of its love to be true to your spirit. What a gift!

One of my best buddies, Vanessa, gave me this fantastic puzzle that's in the form of an elephant. I love it because elephants, as spiritual symbols, hold the power to move through all obstacles. This sounds a little gross, but the other reason I love this puzzle is because, when you pull the elephant's eyes out, the puzzle falls apart. This quirky little object lesson minds me, literally, that when we are willing to see the truth within, the illusion dissolves.

The basic idea is this: if we are truly ready to see who and what we are in the world then the world can truly reveal itself to us.

You can consider the following as you work in this area:

Stop:
- ✓ Trying to stay ahead of your emotions.
- ✓ Needing to understand everything before you allow life to happen.
- ✓ Thinking that you have to have a handle on life before you start to live it.
- ✓ Self-protecting.
- ✓ Thinking you won't be able to handle it when life happens.
- ✓ Holding on to your pain.
- ✓ Keeping yourself in a holding pattern because you don't want to take risk.
- ✓ Listening to self-doubt.
- ✓ Resisting or clinging to life.
- ✓ Needing others to protect you.
- ✓ Creating reasons you can't be in the now.
- ✓ Daydreaming about life and wishing it was different without taking action to make it so.
- ✓ Imposing the life "should" be different rule.
- ✓ Thinking anyone else has to live your life for you.

Start:
- ✓ Looking at your beliefs and make sure they are in reality.
- ✓ Trusting life and what it brings.
- ✓ Embodying your purpose.
- ✓ Sitting with what is uncomfortable.
- ✓ Trusting yourself, know that you can handle what comes your way.
- ✓ Letting emotions move through you when challenges come up.
- ✓ Getting in alignment with how you really feel.
- ✓ Taking it one day at a time.
- ✓ Believing that life is meant to flow naturally.
- ✓ Anticipating a brilliant life.
- ✓ Loosening your control on life.
- ✓ Embracing the pushes of life as a reminder to move.
- ✓ Entering into a new realm.

Make a list of the areas you struggle with the most.
1.
2.
3.
4.
5.

What steps will you take to improve those areas?
1.
2.
3.
4.
5.

How will your life be different when you implement these changes?
_____
_____
_____
_____
_____

Take an honest assessment of where you stand in these areas

Scoring guide:

1 = I realize there's a problem

2 = I have contemplated the issue

3 = I have considered actions steps for the issue

4 = I am prepared to take action

5 = I am taking necessary action steps

6 = I am taking action and I have already made some mistakes

7 = I am integrating lessons from failed action steps

8 = I am making adaptations to my actions

9 = I am being consistent in the actions needed

10 = I am at my ideal goal, I just need to maintain it

Mastering Love

CHAPTER NINE

Zone Modifying

Zone modifying is another necessary stage that must take place if you are going to expand your essence and become your whole being. As you can imagine, when you are wounded you constrict, and when you are healthy you expand. Now that you are taking these steps towards success, it just makes sense that the protective walls that you have created will no longer serve you. You need more room to grow.

As you overcome each of these areas, you will find that you will be filled with more and more strength and confidence. Think of your anxiety as excitement as you approach these doorways. And as you do, you will see a successful completion to all your hard work.

Comfort Zones

We must all face the limiting beliefs and experiences we have accumulated in our life. Through this process, we move toward our higher self and start reuniting with the expansive self rather than the limited, fear-based self. This is such an exciting process, but we desperately avoid it as if it were torture.

To really get to the core of what you are, you need to look at your wounded, neglected parts. Think of your comfort zones as temporary fixes that were placed around you by yourself or others who cared about you when you were hurt. This was done so you could "survive" the disturbance. But now the challenge has passed and you need to remove the protective shield so you can "thrive" again. If you don't, you will stay in your protective shipyard and never sail the sea.

This all makes sense. So why do we struggle with comfort zones? The reason is that we are all trying to avoid the pain that is trapped within us and our ego tries to protect itself from pain or trauma we've experienced in the past. We need a process that will allow us to move beyond the ego limitations of protection and back into the world of evolution.

I have created a process, or theory, called "Essence Illumination" from my experience as a therapist. It is designed to help people awaken after trauma and move beyond their limited perspective of the world. This is one of the key concepts discussed in the theory. If you will not face these doors of change, you will find yourself playing small and living a limited life. Illuminate your essence! Show the world who you are.

I grew up in a home that did not have much money. Travel was seen as an extreme expense and we never had "extra" for that kind of thing. In my later years I've learned to prioritize travel, even when money is tight. Each and every time I return from a trip, I am different. My perspectives change and my fears decrease. I see that I am capable; I see that I am able to expand and that it is safe.

The gift is that when I take others on similar adventures, I see them wake up in the same way. If you get stuck in the same mindset you will never see that there are other possibilities. Comfort zones are just places of refuge that you never left. Think of it like a combat zone and you sought protection in a bomb shelter. What a gift at the time, but if you never leave it, even when the war is over, you will continue to live in the painful memories of the past and in fear. There is no life there, just surviving.

Don't just survive. Thrive!

Tip: Make a list of what you have always wanted to do in life and start there. Soon the ones that are farther from your comfort zones won't seem as far.

To explore this area, consider the following:

Stop:
- ✓ Doing what you did the day before (and before that and before that).
- ✓ Over-thinking everything.
- ✓ Creating possibilities of failure and worrying.
- ✓ Occupying yourself with things that keep you busy so you don't see that you are stuck.
- ✓ Focusing on concerns. Instead, focus on potential.
- ✓ Gossiping and judging others. Focus on yourself instead.
- ✓ Talking about how "someday" things will be different.
- ✓ Over-generalizing that everything is bad.
- ✓ Underestimating your capabilities to overcome adversity.
- ✓ Doing only what you have already experienced.

Start:
- ✓ Doing new things.
- ✓ Asking other people what they love to do.
- ✓ Moving forward, even if it is hard.
- ✓ Implementing plans around your dreams to make them come true.
- ✓ Joining new groups.
- ✓ Testing your capabilities.

✓ Moving past what you think makes you ok.
✓ Changing your routine.
✓ Making a bucket list and doing it.
✓ Creating new places of refuge that you can move in and out of at will.

Make a list of the areas you struggle with the most.
1.
2.
3.
4.
5.

What steps will you take to improve them?
1.
2.
3.
4.
5.

How will your life be different when you implement these changes?

_____
_____
_____
_____
_____

Facing Your Fears

Fear and excitement have a very similar feel in the body. But excitement is something you move towards and fear is something you move away from. This charge in the body alerts you that there is something to be revealed. Remember that on the other side of your greatest fear is your greatest truth. If you can gain the courage to move towards these feelings, you can regain the aspects of the self that have severed.

There are two types of fear. The first is FEAR: Ḟalse Ėvidence Ȧppearing Ṟeal and the other is just healthy fear – the one that is evoked when you are in real danger. You have to stop and look inward first and take an objective view of your external world to truly make a good judgment call as to which type of fear is speaking to you. The gift of doing so is that you will finally see where you are holding yourself back and where the Universe is actually warning you to go a different direction. This can be a very challenging process but also one of the most rewarding.

In my office I teach this concept using a candle as an object lesson. If you move towards the candle and stop over the flame, it will burn you. If you move at a consistent

> *By facing your fears, you find your inner strength to become what you were created to be.*

pace without hesitation, it can sterilize or cleanse what moves through it.

This is the key to healing fear within the body. Move forward without hesitation and trust yourself to manage the challenge as you move through the problem. In the end, you clear the mind, body and spirit. As the fear is released, your life returns to wholeness.

I have also found this to be true: some of my greatest fears were death, public speaking, losing control, and being transparent. Facing my fear in each one of those areas has given me incredible freedom and peace. My career is all about teaching people to let go, to be authentic, and to have faith in the infinite self.

I know now that I have a greater message for the world and that I need to express it in whatever way I can. Nothing will stop me. You too have great wisdom behind those fears that is ready to be revealed. Let go and start moving. Healing is on the way!

Tip: Make a list of your fears. Take one of those fears and create a plan to approach it, address it and to move beyond it. This will amaze you, as your fears are usually nothing like your mind had made them out to be. Addressing your fear is almost always easier than you thought.

To learn more about healthy fear, consider the following:

Stop:
- ✓ Avoiding things that scare you.
- ✓ Thinking that you can't handle it.
- ✓ Believing you are in the original wound. You are far more equipped now than when you were in your childhood.
- ✓ Trying to convince people you can't do things.
- ✓ Making decisions from fear.
- ✓ Working so hard by sidetracking the issue.
- ✓ Making stories up in your mind for why you can't move forward.
- ✓ Focusing on other people's problems, rather than working on your own.
- ✓ Making excuses for why you aren't capable. You are capable.
- ✓ Complaining. Create the life you want. Complaining is suffering and suffering is created. That is a waste of your energy.
- ✓ Thinking you are not worthy of success.
- ✓ Believing that your fear is something you can't overcome.
- ✓ Holding on to fear like it is a part of who you are.

Start:
- ✓ Making an inventory of your fears.
- ✓ Moving toward your fears.
- ✓ Believing you can heal your fears.
- ✓ Replacing fear with the strength and bravery that comes from facing your fears.
- ✓ Looking for patterns that you keep repeating.
- ✓ Making a decision to move forward regardless of the obstacles.
- ✓ Trusting that you were made to get past these barriers.
- ✓ Remembering that you are loved and that suffering is not love. Move beyond the pain.
- ✓ Taking fears apart one at a time.
- ✓ Developing strategies for success.
- ✓ Asking people to support you and hold love around you as you move forward.

Make a list of the areas you struggle with the most.
1.
2.
3.
4.
5.

What steps will you take to improve those areas?
1.
2.
3.
4.
5.

How will your life be different when you implement these changes?

_____

_____

_____

_____

_____

Letting Go of Control

Control is really all about fear. The only reason we even try to control things is because we are trying to manage situations we think we can't handle. Think of it like putting your arms out in front of you and closing your eyes. You swat at everything that crosses your path so you don't have to run into (feel) anything that gets near your vulnerable body. This is a waste of energy and, if continued at length, will only lead to exhaustion of the mind, body, and spirit.

You want to use your energy in a productive, streamlined way. Allow your energy to come in and support you. Trust that you are capable of handling life.

Think of your heart as a filter. It needs to stay open, keeping what serves you and allowing what doesn't to pass. Remember,

> *Control is the belief that you're all-powerful. Who wants that responsibility?*

if you don't stay vulnerable, all you will do is build up toxins and weigh yourself down. Instead of the good things you seek from being closed down, you end up missing all of the sweetness of life and never learning your lessons.

We should also distinguish between healthy control and unhealthy control. Healthy control is when you focus on what will help you grow. Unhealthy control is when you focus on what won't help you grow. It's that simple.

Unhealthy control is really weird when you think about it, but it's also quite common. We can develop a deep desire, for example, to have control over other people's thoughts. You can't make people think the way you want them to, so stay in your own thoughts. It will empower you to grow in your own life. To focus on their thoughts will make you leave your life and lose your way.

One way to maintain healthy control over something is choosing to be intentionally vulnerable. Nothing can ever stop you when your heart is open and you don't cling or resist anything. You just grow. What a blessing!

Think of the word "become." When you become something, there's something from behind pushing you forward. You're like a plant, fed from the earth, bursting into bloom.

When you're "doing" life, you're working with resistance. You're trying to gain strength by proving to the world that you're right. Just become.

Nature always chooses the path of least resistance and the most efficient way. This is evident in the manner in which an apple drops straight to the ground from a tree or how bees create their honeycombs. Nature knows that the hexagonal shape of the combs is the most efficient architecture for reducing wasted space between the cells; plus, building this way requires the least amount of resources. Amazing! Model your life and healing after natural laws like these. Simple and efficient.

Finally, keep in mind that there are two types of work. The first type involves exerting ourselves in a healthy and useful way. This kind of work creates positive outcomes. The second consists of distractions, where we work to keep ourselves busy. Ultimately this leads to unfulfilling outcomes and exhaustion. Letting go of control is positive work.

Tip: Make a decision to release control. Go out for the day and allow life to happen without taking any steps to alter reality. Do this and notice the shifts and changes that occur when you allow flow to return to your life. Allow room for grief, anger, joy, change and new opportunities to show up.

To explore this area more, consider the following:

Stop:
- ✓ Thinking the world needs to make you comfortable.
- ✓ Adapting life events so you can create the outcome you want rather than make sure it is in the best interest of the greater whole.
- ✓ Over-involving yourself in useless life tasks because you are too afraid to try something new.
- ✓ Waiting for what you are afraid of.
- ✓ Quitting when something challenging comes up.
- ✓ Talking about reasons why you can't.
- ✓ Looking for barriers rather than opportunities.
- ✓ Focusing on what you don't want.
- ✓ Being stubborn.
- ✓ Avoiding.

Start:
- ✓ Allowing life to guide you.
- ✓ Moving forward.
- ✓ Releasing any stagnant emotions that come up.
- ✓ Exiting out of situations that don't serve you.
- ✓ Embracing your new aspects of yourself that are coming in.
- ✓ Working on the new aspects of yourself and strengthen them.
- ✓ Seeing through chaos and having faith that you can create a different reality.
- ✓ Looking for opportunities to rise above your challenges.
- ✓ Releasing fear.
- ✓ Seeing control as a prison and move towards freedom.
- ✓ Loving others as they are and letting go of the need to make them different.

Make a list of the areas you struggle with the most.
1.
2.
3.

4.

5.

What steps will you take to improve those areas?

1.

2.

3.

4.

5.

How will your life be different when you implement these changes?

_____

_____

_____

_____

_____

<u>Vulnerability</u>

You've picked up on this already, but when it comes to growth, vulnerability is required. To evolve, you have to open yourself to infinite possibilities, both the positive <u>and</u> the negative experiences of life.

Keep in mind that for some, taking in the positives is just as terrifying as taking in the negatives. Either way you have to learn to let go of control and allow life to flow through you and from you. That gives you an ability to expand and grow no matter what stimuli you receive.

> *Only through brave vulnerability do you expose the real you.*

Vulnerability is a green light to freedom; fear is a big red stop light to everything.

Think of vulnerability as a choice, one that allows you to free your spirit and to dive into a world of possibilities. Don't be afraid of this freedom. Trust that it is a gift of strength.

This is what usually twists people a bit. They think vulnerability equates to weakness. It's not! If you can stay vulnerable in crisis, you can let life pass. If you close up, you hold pain and suffering in. Do you see the gift?

Life passes when you allow it to flow. When you hold on to it, it dams up and creates pressure that must be released in order to heal. Awaken! Letting life pass allows you to live strong and not be held back.

Please remember that vulnerability **MUST** be a choice. If it is forced, it will be painful, and when we feel pain our automatic reaction will be to contract. If this happens to you, turn your **reaction** to a **response**. Choose to face pain and to let it pass. Don't fight it. Let it move through you and become a thing of the past.

When some of my old childhood trauma came up, I used to use this principle in the wrong way but later I understood the lesson. On one of these occasions, someone pushed me to the point where I felt complete and utter despair. I felt I had no value. It seemed like the more I felt bad about myself, the more I wanted to fight, but that only made things worse.

I know now that I allowed myself to be pushed to that point because I wasn't utilizing my resources; I wasn't standing in my value and worth. What I needed to do was realize that when something didn't feel right, I could let go. When I finally gave myself permission to choose, I could decide to let go. My spirit soared!

The lesson learned was that my desire to fight kept me stuck in a victim mentality, which is a disempowered state. Choosing to be vulnerable, regardless of the circumstance, was the key to allowing my spirit to fly.

Tip:
If you are willing to show your "**real**" emotions, being vulnerable becomes a way for others to see you are congruent and trustworthy.

If you want to explore this concept more, consider the following:

Stop:
- ✓ Thinking you have to be strong.
- ✓ Believing you have to do it all.
- ✓ Trying to prove to the world that you are the one with the answers.
- ✓ Trying to hide your true intentions.
- ✓ Thinking it's not safe to express your truth.
- ✓ Telling yourself a story that you are unwanted.
- ✓ Believing that you have nothing to offer the world.
- ✓ Preoccupying your time with distractions so you don't have to expose the real you.
- ✓ Thinking that part of you has to be strong before you expose it.
- ✓ Avoiding troubled waters. Great sailors aren't made by calm waters.
- ✓ Hiding behind false perfection, allow yourself to be seen.
- ✓ Creating any reason to not show up. No more excuses, no more conditions.
- ✓ Talking about it, act upon it instead.

Start:
- ✓ Embracing your vulnerability.
- ✓ Being proud of who you are.
- ✓ Boldly embodying and shine your true inner self.
- ✓ Releasing perfection and shining in your human perfection.
- ✓ Allowing others in.
- ✓ Approving of yourself, so you don't need to seek approval from others.
- ✓ Doing things different. Habits are a way to hide your vulnerability.
- ✓ Living a healthy life so that you can allow your inner light to shine beautifully.
- ✓ Allowing your innocence to shine. The authentic self doesn't need to look smart.
- ✓ Standing in love, which is true strength.
- ✓ Releasing your fears and take a risk by standing in who you are.

✓ Using positive self-talk to remind you of who you really are. The core is always beautiful.

✓ Honoring your own life by allowing others to live their own.

Make a list of the areas you struggle with the most.
1.
2.
3.
4.
5.

What steps will you take to improve those areas?
1.
2.
3.
4.
5.

How will your life be different when you implement these changes?

_____

_____

_____

_____

_____

Boundaries

Boundaries are guidelines, rules, and limits that you create to stay safe. It's how you relay to others, how you need them to behave and respect you. It also clearly tells others what your response to those behaviors will look like when they step past those boundaries.

It sounds so easy, but don't be fooled. This is a hard one. Your current boundaries are based on conclusions you have made throughout life, as well as beliefs, attitudes, and opinions based on past experiences. When information comes from that many places it's bound to be twisted up and confusing.

Fine-tuning this area of your life will create a deep sense of value and self-worth for you, as well as others. People should be able to see that you are a stable, self-reflecting, aware person who values yourself and others. This only happens if clear boundaries are in place.

Want a quick test for clear boundaries? Look at your average relationships. Are they distant? Perhaps your boundaries are too vague to let people get close. You can't risk them crossing the invisible line. Are your closest relationships enmeshed? Then perhaps you have no boundaries and you've lost yourself in the process. The goal is to have relationships that are supportive and loving. Sometimes just a little re-calculating is the trick to getting proper boundaries set.

> *Boundaries are the guidelines to remind us where we're going. When they're unclear, getting lost is a natural consequence.*

Slow down and notice what is uncomfortable in your body. When you're in a situation that makes you uncomfortable, pay attention to the feelings you have. I know my boundaries are compromised when I feel like something toxic is inside me and I want it OUT! That's my flashing red light that someone has crossed my line or, sadly, I have compromised my own line.

Please take on the responsibility of keeping yourself safe and loved. If you don't, all of your other work will be sabotaged. You are precious and it is your job to represent "you."

Ugh! Taking responsibility—God, how I wanted this to be someone else's job. I think the little girl in me, who always wanted to feel protected, donated the job of responsibility to the goodwill of mankind. I had to do a lot of digging in the bins of the warehouse of myself to pull those resources back.

Now as I see my ship come into harbor, if I feel myself being depleted, I take personal responsibility to hold myself and all the work that I've done as sacred. I become acutely aware, address issues directly and do whatever I need to do to secure and safeguard everything that I have worked so hard for as I have maneuvered the seas. If something comes to threaten me or my environment becomes too shallow in what it has to offer me, I embrace the responsibility and navigate my ship accordingly.

Remember that boundaries are your job, not anyone else's. And if you're going to protect what's rightfully yours, you have a door that you can hold sacred when need be.

Tip: It's no one else's job to hold your boundaries. Don't think you can just tell someone and hope they will follow. Your actions are what will confirm that your word is your bond.

For more growth in this area, you can:

Stop:
- ✓ Thinking people crossing your boundaries is somehow a confirmation that you are not good enough.
- ✓ Tolerating being de-valued.
- ✓ Avoiding addressing issues.
- ✓ Thinking its okay to violate someone else's boundaries because they violated yours.
- ✓ Holding people to standards you are unwilling to live by yourself.
- ✓ Trying to act like you are okay with something that isn't okay.
- ✓ Thinking that you have to be nice and you can't hurt someone's feelings.
- ✓ Thinking that you have to be confrontational to have boundaries.
- ✓ Believing that other people don't want boundaries. They do; it helps them feel safe.
- ✓ Thinking people can see your boundaries without you standing in them.
- ✓ Compromising your value because you are ashamed of who you are.

✓ Being afraid of letting people wait until you get clear on what you need.

✓ Believing that it is love to let people cross your boundaries.

✓ Thinking that your coping strategies will last forever.

Start:

✓ Stepping up to the plate and letting the world know how valuable you are.

✓ Valuing yourself. Give yourself permission to raise the bar of love in your life.

✓ Naming your limits.

✓ Tuning into your feelings.

✓ Addressing issues directly.

✓ Practicing becoming more self-aware.

✓ Making self-care your number one priority.

✓ Talking to people who love you and would want to see you valued.

✓ Taking small steps towards the bigger issues. One day at a time until the day you are in total alignment with your heart's desires.

✓ Allowing yourself to take risks and showing how you really feel.

✓ Trusting your heart.

✓ Moving forward and believe that no matter what you face you will be successful.

✓ Trusting that it is in your best interest, as well as everyone else's.

✓ Wanting rather than withholding.

Make a list of the areas you struggle with the most.

1.
2.
3.
4.
5.

What steps will you take to improve those areas?

1.
2.

3.
4.
5.

How will your life be different when you implement these changes?

_____

_____

_____

_____

_____

Take an honest assessment of where you stand in these areas

Scoring guide:

1 = I realize there's a problem

2 = I have contemplated the issue

3 = I have considered actions steps for the issue

4 = I am prepared to take action

5 = I am taking necessary action steps

6 = I am taking action and I have already made some mistakes

7 = I am integrating lessons from failed action steps

8 = I am making adaptations to my actions

9 = I am being consistent in the actions needed

10 = I am at my ideal goal, I just need to maintain it

Zone Modifying

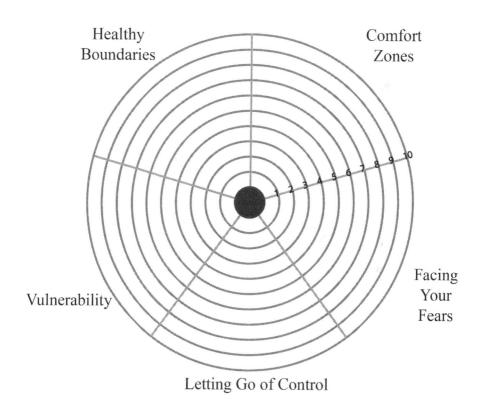

CHAPTER TEN

Integrating and Honoring the World Around You

Creating a Personal Relationship with Your Home

It doesn't matter if you live in a mansion or a box—if you don't love where you reside, you are denying yourself a basic need. Your home represents you and the place that you go to feed your soul. I'm sure many of you are already saying to yourself, "I must be WAY out of balance here because my family doesn't get along, my house is in shambles, and I don't even want to go home." Bingo! That means you have some work to do here.

The home is a representation of your internal state. If your house is in chaos, it's likely that your internal world is as well. If you are hoarding, that can mean you are holding something in and afraid to let go. If your house is in total order, everything has a place and nothing can be disturbed without you losing your cool, it probably means that you are over-controlling.

Controlling behaviors come from fear or the sense you're out of control, so you over-compensate and control your external world. If your internal world was acknowledged, loved, and accepted, how might your home reflect it? When the light of our life is allowed to shine through, we radiate beauty, confidence, security, and hope. So I ask you, how can your home reflect your beauty, confidence, security, and hope?

> *Your environment is a prerequisite for health or sickness.*

We have to stop needing something outside of ourselves to be who we are meant to be. We need to go inward to explore and discover the true perfection of our authentic self. As you shift inward, your external environment will improve. You should consider making changes in your home to reflect your inner beauty. I want your internal and external worlds to align.

Family is crucial to your state of balance. If the relationship between yourself and those in your family is off, you will find your home becomes a prison. So make sure your relationships are supporting you or you may want to make some changes.

Tip: Try doing the opposite of what you are doing and your issues will become really clear.

Here are some practical steps to help you grow in this area:

Stop:
- ✓ Requiring that your home needs to look one way.
- ✓ Pretending things don't bother you and ignoring when your house is out of balance.
- ✓ Overcompensating for what is missing inside you by making your home BIGGER and BETTER.
- ✓ Filling cabinets with all your unfinished business.
- ✓ Blaming others for what a mess your home is.
- ✓ Thinking someone else is responsible for your happiness in your home.
- ✓ Expecting others to be like you.
- ✓ Addressing pain in the home with shame.
- ✓ Emotionally vomiting on others. Projection destroys families and friendships.

✓ Approaching others with a charge. Wait until your emotions pass before addressing issues.

✓ Gossiping or breaking others down because of your own fear of addressing issues.

✓ Aligning with other people because you can't stand in your truth.

✓ Judging others because you don't want to look at yourself.

Start:

✓ Acknowledging the needs of everyone. Remember everyone is equal.

✓ Looking at why you give yourself permission to not be your best at home when you do at work or vice-versa.

✓ Discussing what your needs are with people.

✓ Standing in your truth with love. Do not adapt from what is right for you.

✓ Creating a safe space to express emotions. Allow the full emotional range.

✓ Acknowledging your home is an extension of you. Love it as you want to be loved.

✓ Speaking with love and know that love is where peace is.

✓ Remembering everyone's voice matters.

✓ Taking time to be home, with family, with yourself.

✓ Making your environment a place that refreshes the spirit.

✓ Bringing music in that raises the vibration of your home and family.

✓ Getting outside help if you can't resolve an issue—a therapist, pastor, or friend that will not align with you but guide you.

✓ Respecting the home and keeping it nice.

✓ Bringing in sacred, honoring things that value you and your life.

✓ Remembering that home is a symbol of the heart.

Make a list of the areas you struggle with the most.

1.

2.

3.

4.

5.

What steps will you take to improve those areas?

1.

2.

3.

4.

5.

How will your life be different when you implement these changes?

_____

_____

_____

_____

_____

_____

Creating a Personal Relationship with Your Finances

Finances seem to be an area in which many of us don't seem to know how to find balance. We let money play such an important role in our lives. We like to hoard it, idealize it, fear it, or long for it. Almost everyone comes to the conclusion that there just isn't enough of it. That is such an illusion!

There is always enough, but when you live in the fear of scarcity you create scarcity. The key to success is putting your desire into the world and then allowing the desire to manifest, taking intentional steps towards your desired goal daily. You want to avoid the extremes of impulsiveness and living in the world of lack. You want to be in universal flow. Faith with intention. So what does that look like?

> *The way we manage our finances is our attempt at building a world out of magic.*

Let the Universe know what your heart desires. Let go of how to get it; let go of when. Trust that your wants and desires are important and that when it is right, they will be granted.

Then take one step each day toward your intentions. Make sure you do not have beliefs that are blocking you from receiving. Watch that left side of the body (the feminine side: receiving). Pain can be an indicator of a block. If you find that you are overdoing it, watch out! That may be the masculine side overcompensating for your feelings of low self-worth. Remember, the Universe wants us to have everything we desire. We are the ones that withhold from ourselves.

Recently we bought a fantastic farm home that has brilliant potential but is also an incredible "fixer-upper" project. Super Lisa thought it would be a great idea to save some money and not hire movers. Did I mention that I had a garage full of rocks I had purchased over the years with the intention of moving them into our retail store? Do you know how heavy rocks are?!

Well, this brilliant strategy of being resourceful was actually at the cost of my body. This was an indicator that I had a bit of a poverty mentality and placed too much emphasis on saving money, only later to realize it was at the cost of my lower back. I still have lessons to learn as well.

As the weeks passed, I found myself having a difficult time sitting and I noticed that I was getting quite wiggly in my seat. While at a spiritual retreat, my intern said, "Lisa, I think you're really injured!"

For some reason, in that moment, it hit home. Super Lisa couldn't save the day. The more I tried to save money, the more I depleted my body. My lower back was a symbol of security. I saw the correlation. The aches and pains in my body were trying to tell me where I was out of balance. I was putting finances before the self. That's a NO-NO! Another lesson learned.

> Tip: Money is meant to be a blessing. Use your money in a way that supports you rather than see it as a burden. Be proactive with your blessings. If you see it as a curse you will be reactive with your spending and run on scarcity rather than fulfillment.

Here are some simple ways to grow in this area:

Stop:
- ✓ Robbing Peter to pay Paul.
- ✓ Over-compensating for lack of something by obsessively trying to work yourself to death.
- ✓ Filling the hole of your heart with external things.
- ✓ Buying things to please or earn the approval of another.
- ✓ Spending when you don't have it.
- ✓ Using money as a distraction from your emotions.
- ✓ Valuing money more than yourself.
- ✓ Thinking money is the answer and that when you get it you will be happy.
- ✓ Expecting someone else to create money for you (co-dependency).
- ✓ Using credit to live beyond your means.
- ✓ Justifying unnecessary things.
- ✓ Judging your mistakes. They were necessary to bring you to the point of change.

Start:
- ✓ Allowing the unfolding of financial challenges. It has been said, "Everything built **outside** of integrity collapses to move back into integrity."

✓ Trusting that you will get what you need if you can be patient and allow the realigning to take place.

✓ Trusting if something is being withheld it is because you have over-valued it and the Universe wants you back in balance.

✓ Realizing time is necessary for the unfolding of what doesn't serve you.

✓ Loving the "parts" of you that money has masked and ignored, leaving you feeling unloved and supported. Love yourself in new ways.

✓ Seeing value in everything and shift the focus from just one possibility of receiving money to infinite possibilities.

✓ Exploring new ways of being creative.

✓ Understanding that clarity comes from confusion. Allow confusion to pass, being with it and not controlling it, then clarity will return.

✓ Remembering that no one is ever created without the ability to connect to everything they ever needed.

✓ Believing in miracles when doubt creeps in, knowing the mind is limited by what it knows, but that the Universe is infinite in its ability to manifest.

✓ Understanding that separation happens as a gift to awaken you to the need to return to oneness. Tap back in.

✓ Embracing love from the Universe.

Make a list of the issues you struggle with the most.

1.
2.
3.
4.
5.

What steps will you take to improve those issues?

1.
2.
3.

4.

5.

How will your life be different when you implement these changes?

_____

_____

_____

_____

_____

<u>Connecting with Friends</u>

Connecting to others is a way to share in our similarity and learn from our differences. This helps stimulate the desire to be more. We do this through a process called mirroring. We see ourselves through others' experience of us. This can be a great gift if we are willing to use it to our advantage.

It can also stretch boundaries. As friends start to show their differences, they mirror back areas of our shadow selves, areas beyond our comfort zones. This offers us an opportunity to see what serves us and what doesn't. We learn about ourselves by seeing friends make mistakes and have successes in their lives.

> *Friendship is to see the similarities in another and to approve.*

We each have unique experiences that create our own map of reality. We then use this map to explore and express our reality. It's great fun to see how our maps compare.

Limited maps keep leading us to the same outcome. This gift of connection with others leads us back to infinite possibilities and opportunities for growth. To see the world from multiple perspectives takes us out of our past and starts creating new ways of experiencing life.

I have like the BEST job in the world—seriously! Do you know how many lenses I get to see the world through? I feel like I'm watching a series of movies and each lens has a story to tell. I see the trials and tribulations, the love gained and the love lost, lessons learned and not learned. I bet you want to become a therapist now, don't you?

The gift of my occupation is that my clients, we might call them "teachers" of my profession, show me about the greater landscape. They reveal to me their beautiful insight and methods of navigating the uncharted territories of life.

Do you see the beauty in others' viewpoints? If you catch yourself judging another, it's probably something about you that's creating this reaction. Maybe you think you have it all figured out. But the one that's acting out in front of you is actually the person who is one step ahead of you.

To develop your connections, consider the following:

Stop:
- ✓ Hiding because the world doesn't feel safe. You need to trust **you** and the only way to do that is to try new experiences whether you succeed or fail. By doing so, you learn to stay true to yourself in those challenging moments.
- ✓ Judging friends or yourself. Love what is!
- ✓ Acting as if you don't need people. We all need people to thrive.
- ✓ Putting on a persona to make connection easier. Be authentic, or you are just creating unreal relationships that will quickly burn out overtime.
- ✓ People pleasing. You are lying to people. You can't expect them to trust you when you aren't being true to yourself.
- ✓ Projecting. Projecting is a way we leak our energy onto someone else because we don't want to deal with something hard. Take responsibility for your being.
- ✓ Dangling "carrots" to get the approval of others. Stop over-giving or over-complementing so they will be attracted to you. Stand in who you are.
- ✓ Shutting yourself down by negative self-talk. Drop "They won't like me" or "I'll never be enough."
- ✓ Forcing your agenda on others or telling them how they should be.

✓ Over-focusing on yourself so you can't see the needs and wants of others.

✓ Letting your fears stop you from being true to your desire for connection.

✓ Acting like you are too smart and everyone else is dumb. We all have value and have something to offer.

✓ Telling yourself you don't relate to people. Differences are what make us unique.

✓ Telling yourself you won't be wanted.

✓ Seeing what is wrong in others. Look for what is right.

✓ Having expectations. Just enjoy people as they are.

Start:

✓ Believing connection is possible. It is always waiting to be made.

✓ Opening up to the possibility of new people in your life.

✓ Becoming curious about others. Ask questions so people can see you are invested in them.

✓ Seeing what is similar and different in you and others.

✓ Reaching out without expectations. Embrace opportunities for true joy and pleasure with others.

✓ Loving life in front of people. Live out loud!

✓ Showing how you really feel. Be totally transparent.

✓ Showing up authentically. Be the real you and you will pull in others who are doing the same. Like minds draw like minds.

✓ Seeing friends as your teammates

✓ Engaging in discussions and play.

✓ Sharing your desires and dreams.

✓ Sharing your story, how you came into this world, and why you see the world the way you do.

Make a list of the areas you struggle with the most.

1.

2.

3.

4.

5.

What steps will you take to improve those areas?

1.
2.
3.
4.
5.

How will your life be different when you implement these changes?

_____

_____

_____

_____

_____

Connecting with Community

Community is an essential part of the greater self. The research is clear that a sense of being and connectedness with the world around us is essential to our overall health. If we look at life as a mirror, then we should note that our community is just an expanded version of ourselves and pure potential.

Your community offers opportunities, lessons, illusions, truth, and entertainment. Each part plays a unique role in your awakening. Community can show up in places you would never expect. It may be a book club, a class at your gym, or a local church. All you *Community helps you see when too much alone time distorts your thinking.* need to do is look for groups that are doing what you love or that you are curious about and join in. The rest will fall into place. Show up and be ready and open for connection.

Early on, I made the decision that I wanted to create a community. I wanted to find like-minded individuals that had interests and loves like me. I started this process by talking out loud about my interests and the things I loved. It didn't take long and I started to notice that people were intrigued by what I was saying. They were eager to share in the process and explore it together.

I started to invite teachers to come to Journeys (our holistic healing center) to educate me more about various things I wanted to know. As I did, others started to follow and we started to share in community. Shortly after, we began creating volunteer opportunities where others could give back to the community just the way I love to. Groups are now expanding and thriving, while opportunities continue to grow as well.

When I made space in my heart for my community, they came. I'm so grateful! These are my dearest and truest friends now. Surround yourself with likeminded people who wanted to grow and discover their fullest potential.

> Tip:
> Do you want to know the real you? If so, start today by expanding your connection to your greater community. Find a group of like-minded people and start building a relationship today.

Here is how you can develop your connection to community:

Stop:
- ✓ Relying on just what you know. Ask others for feedback.
- ✓ Being overly independent. Time alone and time with others is equally important. Balance is the answer.
- ✓ Believing that community isn't safe. Community is pivotal in balancing one's life.
- ✓ Interpreting others and just let them be.
- ✓ Putting conditions on others. Let them show you who they really are.
- ✓ Transposing your beliefs onto others. Enjoy the blending of others.

✓ Keeping yourself imprisoned in your own home. Reach out.

✓ Allowing your insecurities to isolate you. Stretch yourself. You are insecure because you are pretending you are not whole.

✓ Envisioning what could go wrong. Just trust it will be as it is meant to be.

✓ Eliciting rejection by believing in it. Let go of the idea that rejection is a bad thing. It's just the Universe's way of saying "wrong door."

✓ Needing approval. This will only delay any real connection because it is conditional.

✓ Having an agenda. Be with what is.

✓ Gossiping. This will make you an untrustworthy member of your community.

✓ Holding yourself back.

Start:

✓ Remembering you are an evolutionary being. Living alone will not stimulate growth.

✓ Incorporating your dreams into your expression of you. People will want to join you.

✓ Looking for what you desire in your world and connect with those who have similar interests.

✓ Interacting with people.

✓ Being willing to play the fool and show your humanness. Others can relate to that.

✓ Showing all of who you are. Again, live transparently.

✓ Inspiring others to be their best.

✓ Trying new things and going out of those comfort zones. That new event may be where you unite with your next community.

✓ Traveling beyond your wildest dreams.

✓ Looking for community in places you love.

✓ Realizing you deserve it!

Make a list of the areas you struggle with the most.

1.

2.

3.

4.

5.

What steps will you take to improve those areas?

1.

2.

3.

4.

5.

How will your life be different when you implement these changes?

_____

_____

_____

_____

_____

Creating a Personal Relationship with the Earth and All Its Creations

It is vitally important to open your heart to all of nature's creations. They are precious and a great gift to us if we honor them. If we do harm to these creations, then we create harm to ourselves. Mother earth is here to support us. All of her creatures hold love and purpose. Don't miss the opportunity to see the value of each and every living thing. You will see the value of yourself mirrored back from their essence.

I worked with a client who struggled with disabilities. I would go to her foster care home to help her navigate life in a more productive way. She had three snakes in her room and would quite often pull them out and have them wind up her arm or around her neck as we worked together. I

> *To invest in relationships with earth and the creatures within it builds a bridge to the one who created you.*

had a great fear of snakes and so I was very proud of myself for being in the room, let alone have them loose on her arm.

One day she said, "I don't understand why people are so afraid of these spiritual animals," and then she put a snake right by my face. My heart started to race and I pulled back quickly. She said, "Lisa, you teach people to open their hearts. How can you close your heart to snakes? They are God's creatures too."

She was right. I let my fear stop me from opening my heart and connecting with a part of the natural world. I was soon able to be with the snakes and touch them. And she was right too, that when I opened my heart, I could see their beauty.

Every gift of the world is meant to be explored with an open heart. If you can't, there is likely a trauma there that you may want to explore to free your spirit. As the Buddhists say, "On the other side of your greatest fear, is your greatest truth." Opening your heart will align you with your higher purpose.

Be at peace with the earth and all of its creatures. Each has a gift of wisdom. Open your mind and what comes of that simple action of release will be something bigger than you could have ever imagined.

We are all unique puzzle pieces in a greater whole. One can exist without the other, but the full picture cannot be enjoyed without the other.

When you open your heart to love another, you open your heart to love yourself. Loving all things creates space for loving all aspects of you as well.

Tip: **Looking up** an animal spirit guide from Native American totems can be a useful tool and may help you work through any limiting beliefs. Also notice if animals cross your path repeatedly, they may be trying to show you something.

Here's how you can grow in this area:

Stop:
- ✓ Living in fear. If you have an animal in the world you don't love, explore its spiritual meaning. See how it relates to you and your life.
- ✓ Acting like you aren't a part of the earth. You are!
- ✓ Over-using or wasting resources.
- ✓ Acting like you don't have time for your animals or the creatures of the world.
- ✓ Acting like there are good and bad animals. All are necessary.
- ✓ Hiding indoors and not embracing nature.
- ✓ Polluting and living like this planet cannot be destroyed. It can!
- ✓ Acting like the earth is full of resources that can never be exhausted.
- ✓ Thinking the earth doesn't need your love as much as you need love from it.
- ✓ Over-using pesticides. They are hard on the environment and if animals ingest them, it can be deadly.

Start:

✓ Facing the parts of nature that you fear and receive the gifts that you are given as you work through it.

✓ Focusing on everything like a child does. Life is awesome when you open your senses again to experience it.

✓ Creating adventure. Seek out new things, opportunities, and new experiences. Never quit!

✓ Being one with the earth. Take your shoes off, get in the garden, watch a sunset.

✓ Consciously breathing.

✓ Looking for AWE-someness! (awe of creation)

✓ Looking for people to share your experiences with.

✓ Touching, tasting, smelling, listening, and looking as you experience your world.

✓ Creating a restorative environment – one that re-creates at least as much as something is consumed.

✓ Finding solutions to deficits, honoring the earth's needs.

✓ Recycling, not wasting.

✓ Using healthy, natural products.

✓ Traveling.

Make a list of the areas that you struggle the most.

1.
2.
3.
4.
5.

What steps will you take to improve those areas?

1.
2.
3.
4.
5.

How will your life be different when you implement these changes?

_____

_____

_____

_____

_____

Loving the World You Are In

We need to fall in love with the world and everything in it. That includes you and me! When we value all things, we raise the value of ourselves.

If you want to come back to your wholeness, you will need to value the world you live in. It will support you as you grow, so in a sense, you are the keeper of the foundation of your life. This love includes everything—the people, the animals, the earth beneath our feet, and the air we breathe. Each and every part is an expression of something much greater than we can understand.

The Universe has the big picture and you have a piece of the puzzle. If you value each piece of the puzzle, they naturally come together. If you do not value a piece of the puzzle, the picture makes no sense.

> *To show love to the earth and everything in it is to honor the sacredness of who you are. To dishonor it is to destroy the resources that sustain you.*

As we gain insight in life, we need to deepen our relationships with the gifts of the world. This is much like valuing the gift of giving birth. When you see the gift of life, you can embrace life in a more profound way. As we navigate each opportunity of our life we gain wisdom and growth.

On the day of your death you have to let go and trust that what you have done was what you were meant to do. You hope to finish well—to have lived a life where you left a legacy. You want to have blessed this world with your life, rather than doing harm that affects future generations. You must value the world that gives you this opportunity and leave it better than when you arrived.

If you do not love and honor your experiences and circumstances, neither gift will be able to remind you how to move forward. The past informs the future. Each moment is the blessing. The world as a whole is a reminder that life is a continuous stream of seasons and experiences. When you understand the cycles of life you understand the value of working in harmony with it.

You were born into this life for a reason. The world and everything in it is here to support you. Are you paying attention to how loved you are or are you looking for ways to take from the world because it owes you? Look for love.

The earth holds the secrets of creation. Kill or damage the earth and in the end it's going to do the same to you. It is an avoidable mistake if you are conscious of your choices.

Tip: Do a beach cleanup or just go around your neighborhood and pick up garbage. Support animal shelters or make sure you recycle at home and at work. Find ways to give back and trust that what you give will be a gift that will pay itself forward.

To grow in this area, consider the following thoughts:

Stop:
- ✓ Littering.
- ✓ Ignoring the long-term effects of our choices to our planet.
- ✓ Acting as if our resources are never going to run out.
- ✓ Believing the world is for our taking.
- ✓ Treating people unequally.
- ✓ Hurting animals.

✓ Thinking others don't matter.
✓ Thinking you don't matter.
✓ Acting as if the cycle of life doesn't exist.
✓ Acting like you don't play an integral role in the health of the earth.
✓ Expecting the earth to feed you without you feeding it.
✓ Only receiving and not giving back.
✓ Polluting.
✓ Being inefficient.

Start:
✓ Replanting.
✓ Creating sustainability.
✓ Supporting the underprivileged.
✓ Leaving no room for injustice.
✓ Treating animals humanely.
✓ Valuing all things.
✓ Creating equality.
✓ Leaving an honoring footprint on the earth.
✓ Recycling.
✓ Believing that you have the power to make change.
✓ Taking action in your community.
✓ Preparing for challenges that may arise, so you can help those who have not.

Make a list of the areas you struggle with the most.
1.
2.
3.
4.
5.

What steps will you take to improve those areas?

1.

2.

3.

4.

5.

How will your life be different when you implement these changes?

_____

_____

_____

_____

_____

<u>Connecting with Those You Want to Be Like – A Hero</u>

Think about those people that you really look up to or have put on a pedestal. Find out what it is in them that makes you feel so good. Now strive to find those character traits within yourself. This is the purpose of heroes.

Know that you are drawn to heroes because they remind you of something already in you. Once you figure out what that is, quickly take those folks off the pedestal before they fall. They will almost certainly fall and when you see them fall (if you haven't done your work) it's likely you will believe you are incapable of accomplishing your dreams because they didn't accomplish theirs.

Remember that you are always good enough. As long as you are in your own light, you can accomplish anything. If you are in someone else's shadow, you will think your light is dim and you will question if you are good enough. So see them, love them, integrate their message, and keep moving on your path. This really makes life so much more enticing. The more I love and am drawn to something, the more I grow.

> *Your heroes are the way that you can personally raise the bar for yourself. See it and then create it!*

A word of caution: If you keep seeing only what sparkles in others and it leads you to stray off your own path, you will forever be lost in others or things. If you see them as a reflection of your higher self and quickly get to the task of integrating those aspects of yourself, you will move straight toward your destiny. Fall in love with the multifaceted you!

Brian, my brother, is a scholarly individual who always baffled me as a child. He was adopted and, unlike the rest of my family—who was all about emotions, connection, and feeling—he came from a world of intelligence and brilliance.

I always appreciated him but in the way a human looks into an aquarium and admires the beautiful fish. I was in awe, but I couldn't quite relate.

When I found my partner, I found someone that thinks more along the same lines as my brother. She, in a way, bridged the relationship between my brother and myself. I found that we are more alike than different; we were meant to go together.

When my emotional IQ and his intellectual IQ begin to work together, the world makes more sense. Through his brilliant observations over the years and my emotional experiences, we find truth in each other's perspectives. We both bring aspects of the color spectrum together to create the full dynamic range of life.

This relationship brings me a greater understanding, one that is rich with adventure and common sense. I love that my brother did the work of learning from the world, while I went on an adventure to experience it. Now when we get together, what a tale we have to tell!

Tip: When you find a hero, observe them and embrace your connection to them. Soak up everything you can. Love them and then love those qualities in yourself.

Consider this as you move forward:

Stop:

✓ Idolizing others. No one is better than you. They are just reminding you of who you are.

✓ Believing you aren't as good as someone else. Get excited when someone sparks your attention. You are on the path to you.

✓ Thinking someone has what you want, but that you are incapable of attaining it.

✓ Wasting your time over-focusing on others to get their approval. You need your approval; that's it. If you can't approve of yourself, then that is what you need to focus on.

✓ Over-stimulating others' egos and under-stimulating your soul.

✓ Believing that your gifts are outside of you. They are inside.

✓ Over-entertaining yourself and not completing enough personal action toward your goals. You've got this, if you would just get to it.

✓ Deliberately creating illusions of worthlessness and acting like other people have what you should have, but don't. You have what you need. Trust it.

✓ Thinking you can't grow. There is always more to you. Go find it.

Start:
- ✓ Embodying your gifts and knowing that you have so much to give the world. All you need to do is embrace them.
- ✓ Engaging in the process of change.
- ✓ Finding how interesting it is that you have your particular gifts and see what you can do with them.
- ✓ Dreaming of your potential and get excited to find the ways to bring it into reality.
- ✓ Being proud that you can see where you are headed.
- ✓ Loving those parts and helping them grow.
- ✓ Translating the gifts you see and bringing them into your own story, manifesting them into the literal new you.
- ✓ Exemplifying them in your life. Give them a way to be expressed in your world.
- ✓ Transcending the illusion of barriers that have stopped you from doing what you see others are succeeding at.
- ✓ Contemplating ways of engaging these traits in multiple expressions.
- ✓ Seeing yourself in this new way in the future. Dream of its perfect manifestation.
- ✓ Cheering yourself on the evolutionary path.
- ✓ Getting excited for the new you!

Make a list of the areas you struggle with the most.
1.
2.
3.
4.
5.

What steps will you take to improve those areas?
1.
2.
3.
4.
5.

How will your life be different when you implement these changes?

_____

_____

_____

_____

_____

CONCLUSION

Now take the score of each section and add it to the chart.

Overall Balance

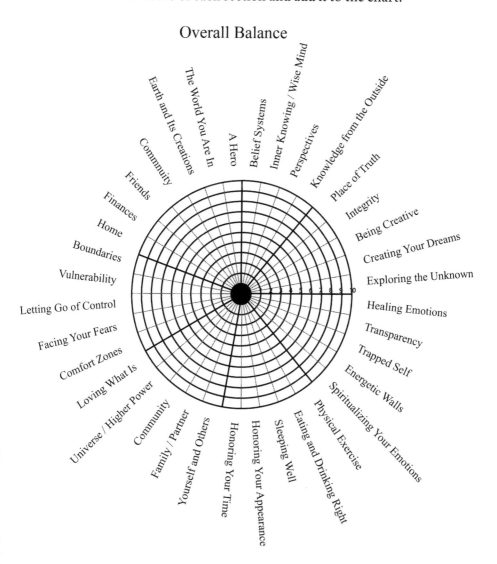

Perhaps without realizing it, you've created a comprehensive chart of you. Included in the chart are the areas that require your attention. The chart is also a clear description of all areas of your life that you need to consider as you are moving towards balance. This will allow you to keep the whole in mind. You will be able to build strength in one area without sacrificing or damaging another.

As each stage is completed, you will unite more intimately with your higher self. Your inner child will feel loved and supported. You'll create a deeper synchronicity of the mind, body, and spirit connection. When these aspects come together, you will find a symphony of rhythm, sensuality, and flow. It's almost like receiving food and water after it has been withheld from you on a hot and physically-taxing day. You can relax and be recharged as life unfolds before you. You can allow yourself to come back to a natural state of peace.

I hope through this whole process that you see that it really comes down to you. You are the one who is in charge—you are 100% responsible for your own destiny. Don't give your power away, don't be tricked into believing that you are powerless or that the responsibility is too heavy. Be grateful for the coping strategy to survive, but you no longer need this in your life. You are ready to live a fantastic, fulfilling life.

Now you are ready to begin the hard work—and benefit from it! By using these concepts for success you will create a balanced, centered life, now and in your future. You will be on the path to align with your purpose. You'll enable yourself to live a great life. No more reasons why you can't be fulfilled. You will address the issues, clear the path, and step into the authentic you.

I want this for you just as much as I want it for myself. This book has been written as a personal journey to find my balance and I give it to you as my blessing to your success. It's the overflow from finding myself and the core of who I am.

When you come to a place on your path where you realize you have found you and your spirit is full, please pass on the lessons to those who seek answers. This is how we feed one another, and how we continue on the path of evolution.

I love that I've gained another friend in you, today. Let's walk together on the path to wholeness.

Blessings to you. May we all be restored to our natural state of balance.

Your friend and teammate,
Lisa

74906650R00120

Made in the USA
Middletown, DE
01 June 2018